FIRST 50
KIDS' SONGS
YOU SHOULD PLAY ON GUITAR

ISBN 978-1-5400-6289-5

HAL•LEONARD®

Visit Hal Leonard Online at
www.halleonard.com

Contact us:
Hal Leonard
7777 West Bluemound Road
Milwaukee, WI 53213
Email: info@halleonard.com

In Europe, contact:
Hal Leonard Europe Limited
42 Wigmore Street
Marylebone, London, W1U 2RN
Email: info@halleonardeurope.com

In Australia, contact:
Hal Leonard Australia Pty. Ltd.
4 Lentara Court
Cheltenham, Victoria, 3192 Australia
Email: info@halleonard.com.au

CONTENTS

Addams Family Theme

Theme from the TV Show and Movie
Music and Lyrics by Vic Mizzy

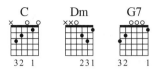

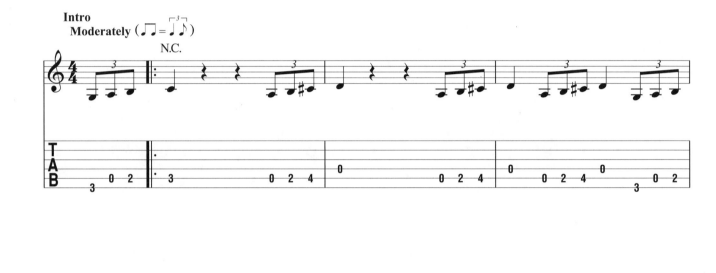

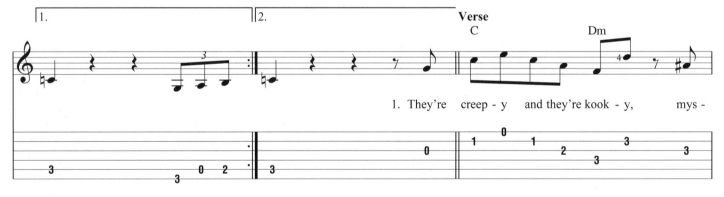

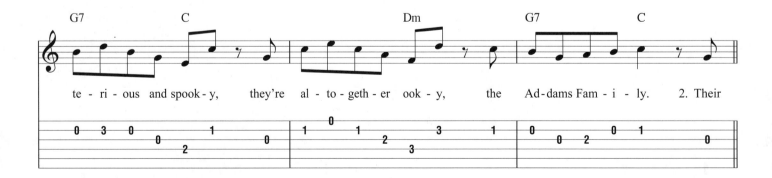

1. They're creep-y and they're kook-y, mys-te-ri-ous and spook-y, they're al-to-geth-er ook-y, the Ad-dams Fam-i-ly. 2. Their

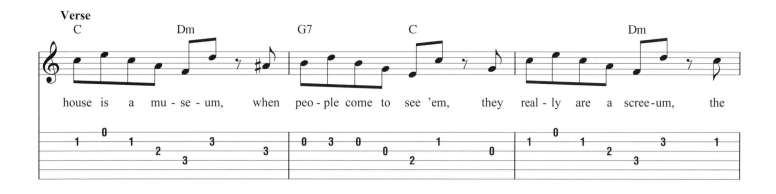

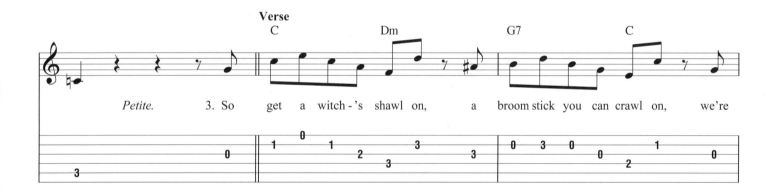

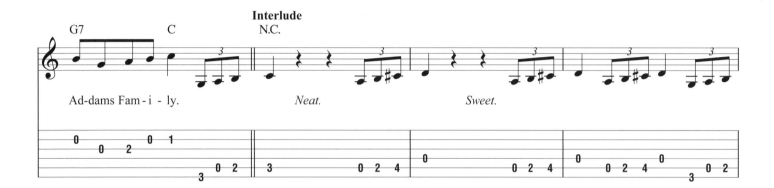

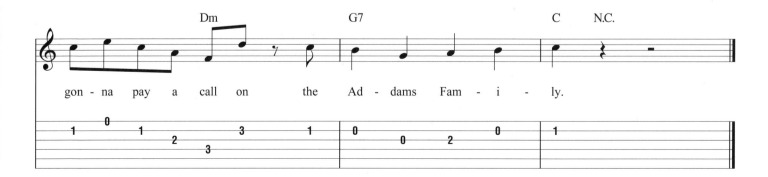

Alphabet Song

Traditional

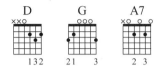

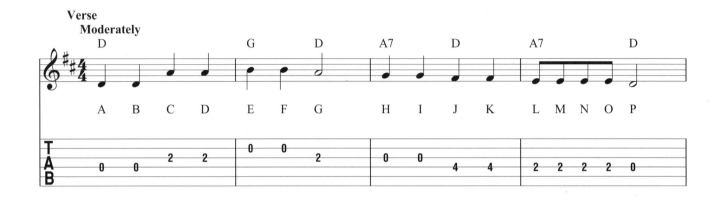

Bananas in Pyjamas

Words and Music by Carey Blyton

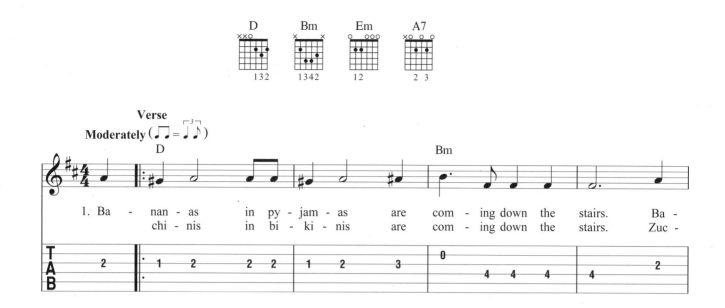

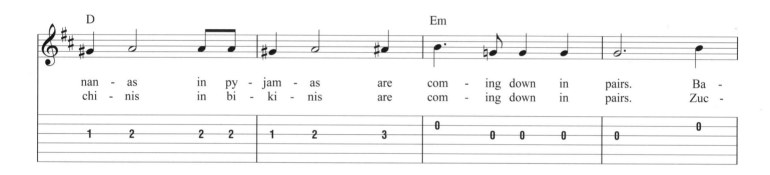

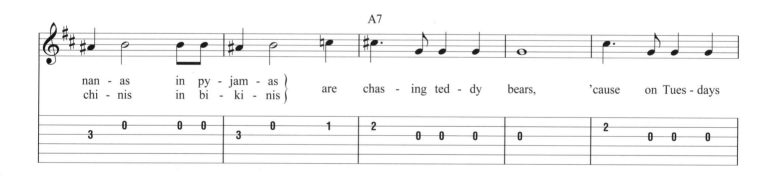

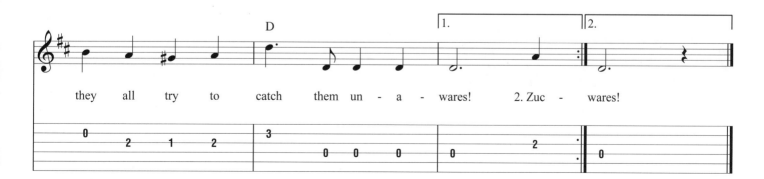

Any Dream Will Do

from JOSEPH AND THE AMAZING TECHNICOLOR® DREAMCOAT

Music by Andrew Lloyd Webber
Lyrics by Tim Rice

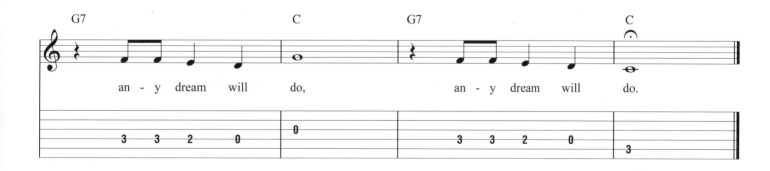

Additional Lyrics

3. May I return to the beginning,
   The light is dimming and the dream is too.
   The world and I, we are still waiting,
   Still hesitating, any dream will do.

Bob the Builder (Main Title)

Words and Music by Paul K. Joyce

Verse

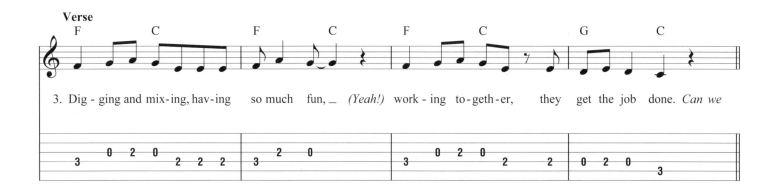

3. Dig - ging and mix - ing, hav - ing   so much fun, __ *(Yeah!)* work - ing to - geth - er,   they get the job done. *Can we*

Pre-Chorus

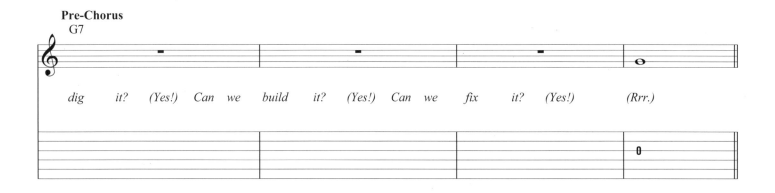

dig   it? (Yes!) Can we build   it? (Yes!) Can we   fix   it? (Yes!)   (Rrr.)

Chorus

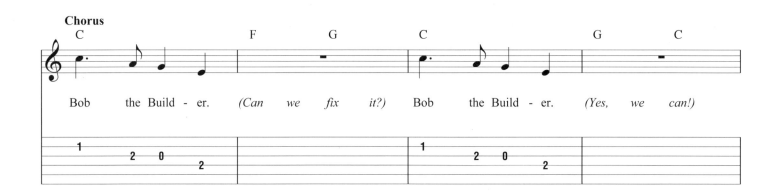

Bob   the Build - er. *(Can   we   fix   it?)* Bob   the Build - er.   *(Yes,   we   can!)*

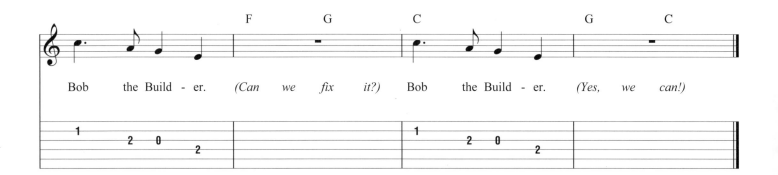

Bob   the Build - er. *(Can   we   fix   it?)* Bob   the Build - er.   *(Yes,   we   can!)*

"C" Is for Cookie

from the Television Series SESAME STREET
Words and Music by Joe Raposo

Additional Lyrics

3. *Spoken: Hey, you know what?*
A round cookie with one bite out of it looks like a C.
A round doughnut with one bite out of it also looks like a C.
But it is not as good as a cookie.
Oh, and the moon sometimes looks like a C, but you can't eat that, so...

The Candy Man

from WILLY WONKA AND THE CHOCOLATE FACTORY

Words and Music by Leslie Bricusse and Anthony Newley

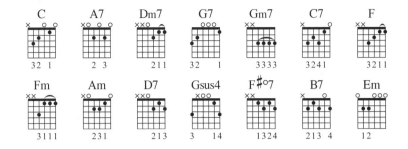

Verse

Moderately, in 2

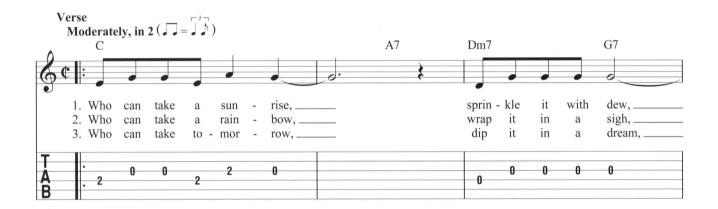

1. Who can take a sun - rise, _____ sprin - kle it with dew, _____
2. Who can take a rain - bow, _____ wrap it in a sigh, _____
3. Who can take to - mor - row, _____ dip it in a dream, _____

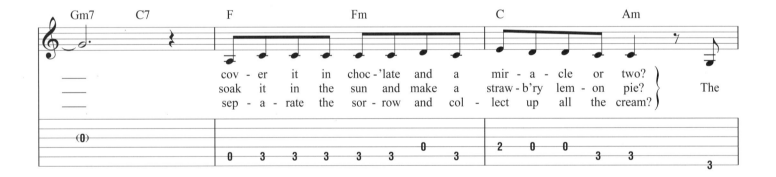

___ cov - er it in choc - 'late and a mir - a - cle or two? }
___ soak it in the sun and make a straw - b'ry lem - on pie? } The
___ sep - a - rate the sor - row and col - lect up all the cream? }

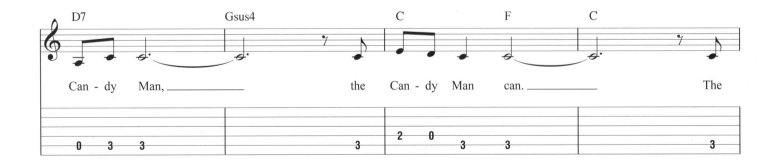

Can - dy Man, _____ the Can - dy Man can. _____ The

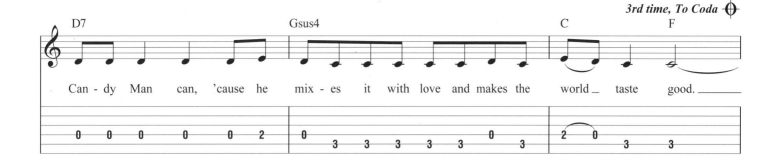
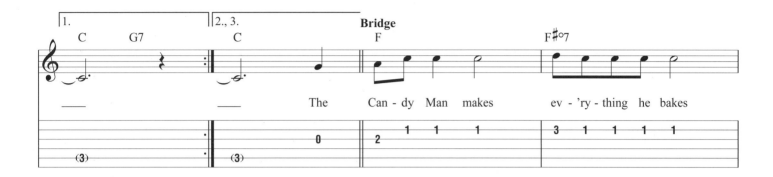
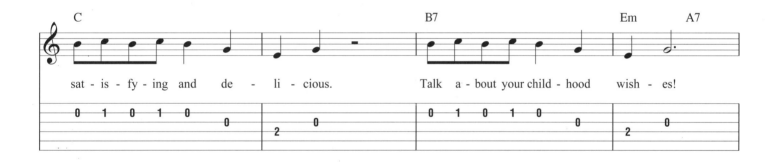
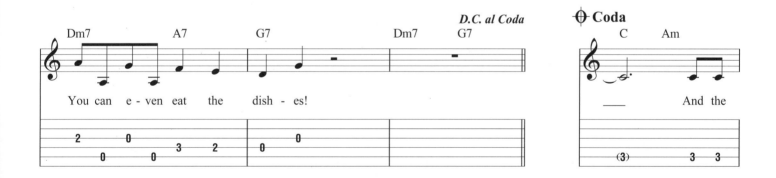
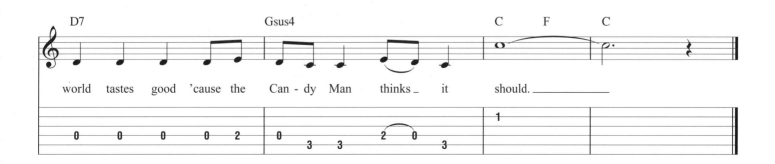

Castle on a Cloud

from LES MISÉRABLES

Music by Claude-Michel Schönberg
Lyrics by Alain Boublil, Jean-Marc Natel and Herbert Kretzmer

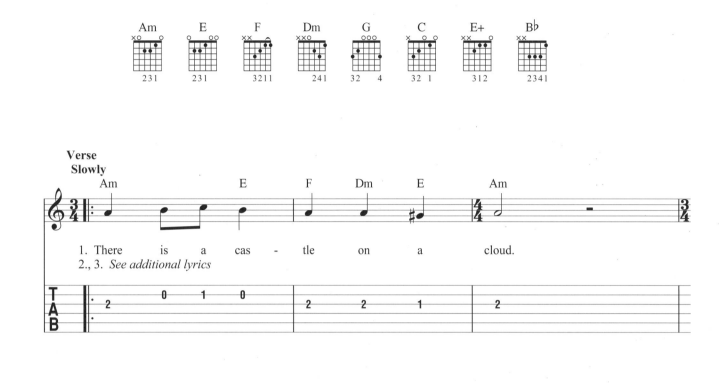

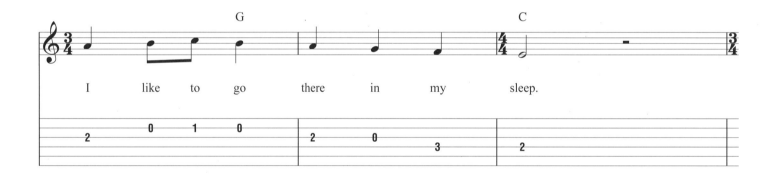

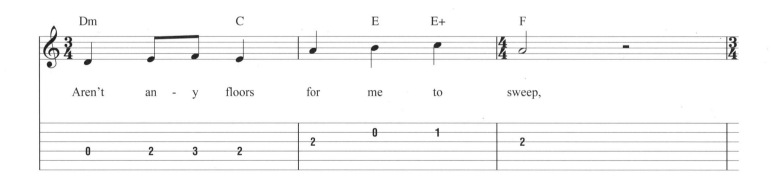

Music and French Lyrics Copyright © 1980 by Editions Musicales Alain Boublil
English Lyrics Copyright © 1986 by Alain Boublil Music Ltd. (ASCAP)
Mechanical and Publication Rights for the U.S.A. Administered by Alain Boublil Music Ltd. (ASCAP) c/o Spielman Koenigsberg & Parker, LLP,
Richard Koenigsberg, 1675 Broadway, 20th Floor, New York, NY 10019, Tel 212-453-2500, Fax 212-453-2550, ABML@skpny.com

Additional Lyrics

2. There is a room that's full of toys.
   There are a hundred boys and girls.
   Nobody shouts or talks too loud,
   Not in my castle on a cloud.

3. I know a place where no one's lost.
   I know a place where no one cries.
   Crying at all is not allowed,
   Not in my castle on a cloud.

The Chicken Dance

By Terry Rendall and Werner Thomas
English Lyrics by Paul Parnes

Additional Lyrics

2. Hey, you're in the swing.
   You're cluckin' like a bird. (Pluck, pluck, pluck, pluck.)
   You're flappin' your wings.
   Don't you feel absurd. (No, no, no, no.)
   It's a chicken dance,
   Like a rooster and a hen. (Ya, ya, ya, ya.)
   Flappy chicken dance;
   Let's do it again.

Chorus 2. Relax and let the music move you.
   Let all your inhibitions go.
   Just watch your partner whirl around you.
   We're havin' fun now; I told you so.

3. Now you're flappin' like a bird
   And you're wigglin' too. (I like that move.)
   You're without a care.
   It's a dance for you. (Just made for you.)
   Keep doin' what you do.
   Don't you cop out now. (Don't cop out now.)
   Gets better as you dance;
   Catch your breath somehow.

4. Now we're almost through.
   Really flyin' high. (Bye, bye, bye, bye.)
   All you chickens and birds,
   Time to say goodbye. (To say goodbye.)
   Goin' back to the nest,
   But the flyin' was fun. (Oh, it was fun.)
   Chicken dance was the best,
   But the dance is done.

Chitty Chitty Bang Bang

from CHITTY CHITTY BANG BANG

Words and Music by Richard M. Sherman and Robert B. Sherman

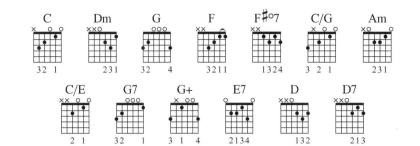

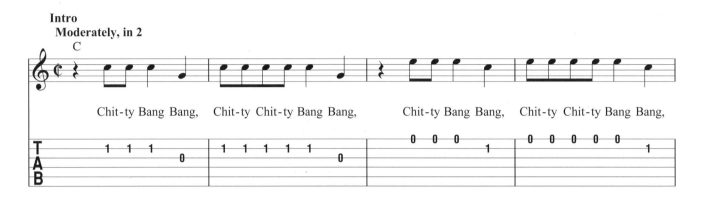

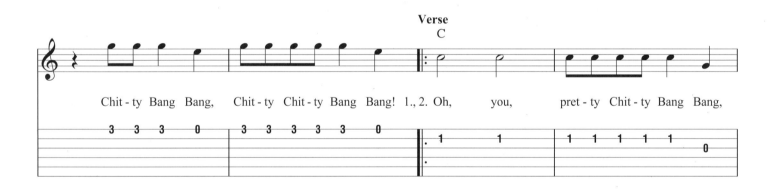

Ding-Dong! The Witch Is Dead

from THE WIZARD OF OZ

Lyric by E.Y. "Yip" Harburg
Music by Harold Arlen

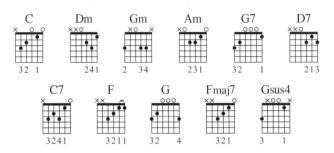

Chorus
Moderately, in 2

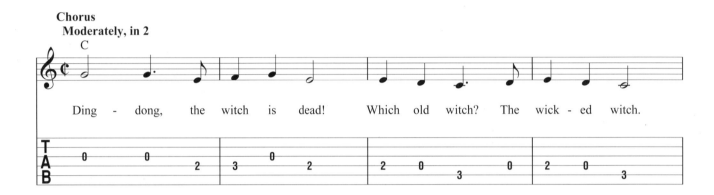

Ding - dong, the witch is dead! Which old witch? The wick - ed witch.

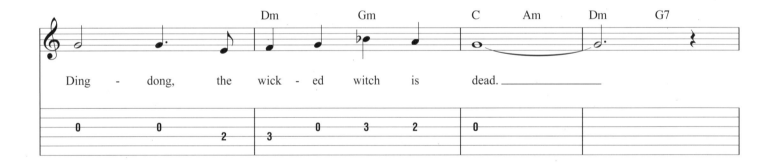

Ding - dong, the wick - ed witch is dead. _____

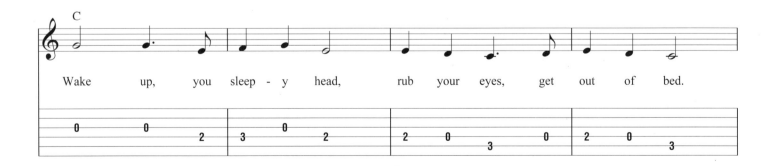

Wake up, you sleep - y head, rub your eyes, get out of bed.

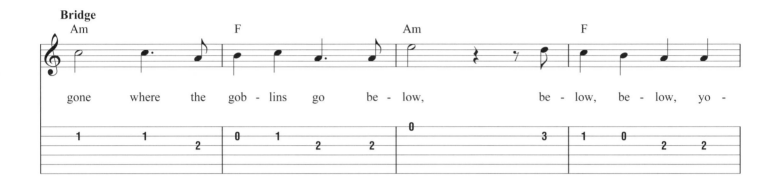

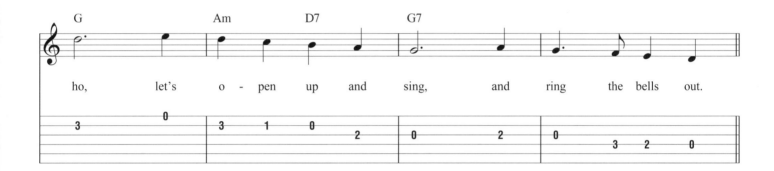

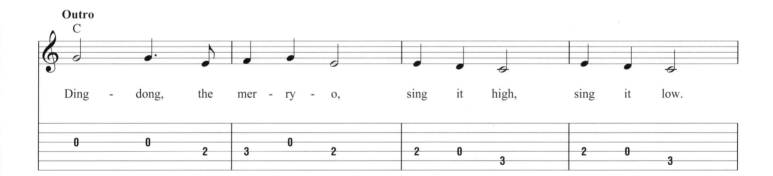

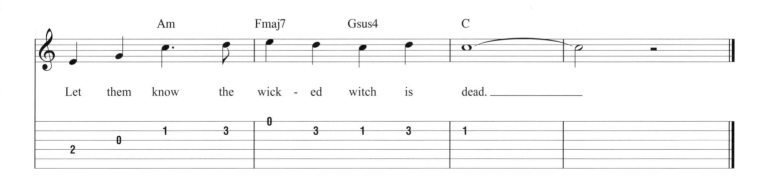

Dites-Moi
(Tell Me Why)

from SOUTH PACIFIC

Lyrics by Oscar Hammerstein II
Music by Richard Rodgers

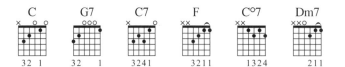

Verse
Moderately

1. Di - tes - moi _____ pour - quoi _____ la vie est bel - le,
2. Tell me why _____ the sky _____ is filled with mu - sic,

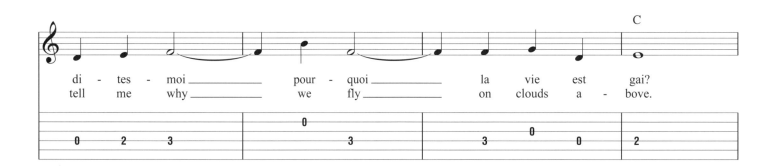

di - tes - moi _____ pour - quoi _____ la vie est gai?
tell me why _____ we fly _____ on clouds a - bove.

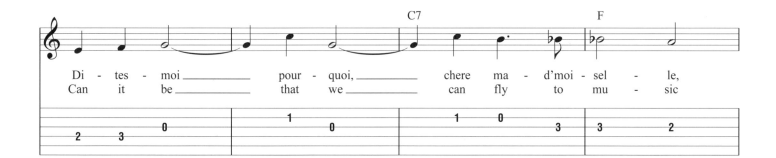

Di - tes - moi _____ pour - quoi, _____ chere ma - d'moi - sel - le,
Can it be _____ that we _____ can fly to mu - sic

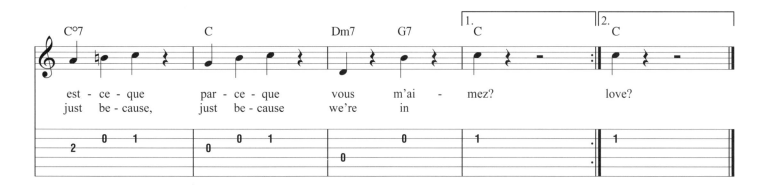

est - ce - que par - ce - que vous m'ai - mez?
just be - cause, just be - cause we're in

1. love?

God Bless America ®

Words and Music by Irving Berlin

Do-Re-Mi

from THE SOUND OF MUSIC
Lyrics by Oscar Hammerstein II
Music by Richard Rodgers

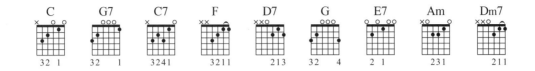

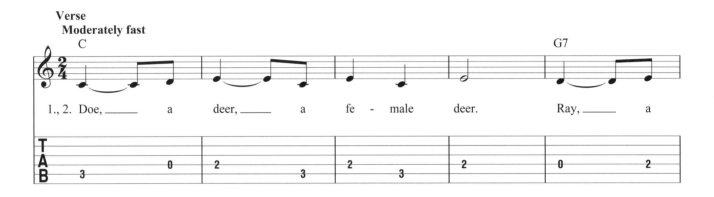

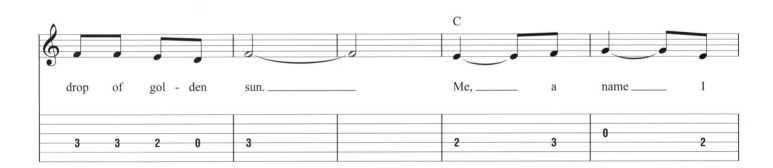

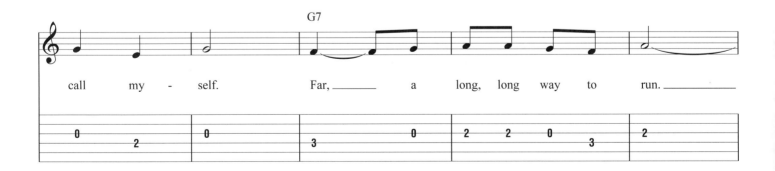

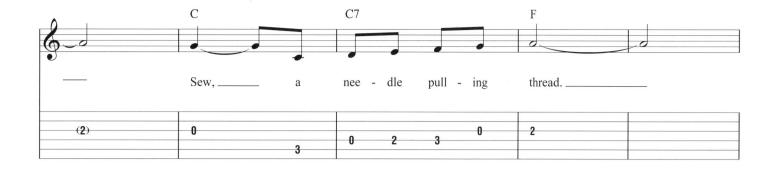

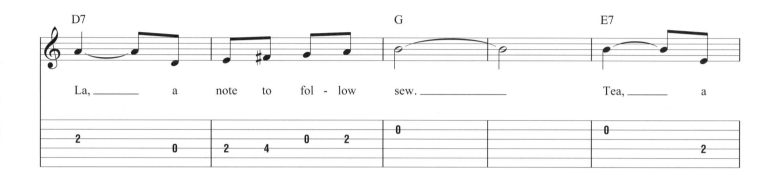

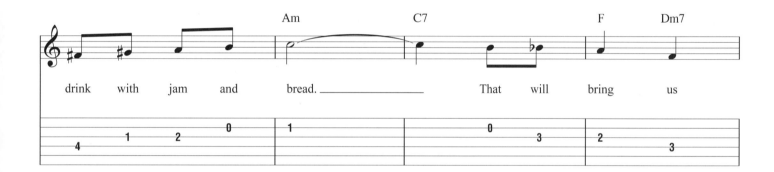

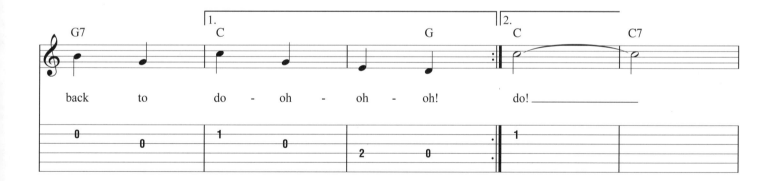

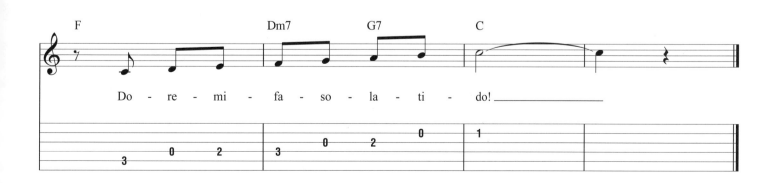

Hakuna Matata

from THE LION KING
Music by Elton John
Lyrics by Tim Rice

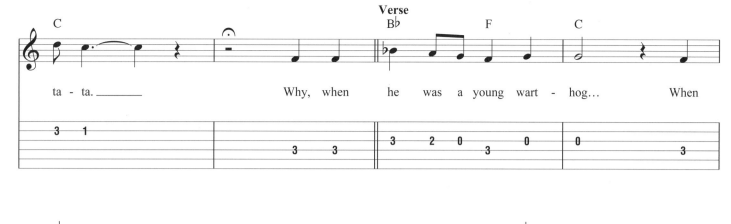

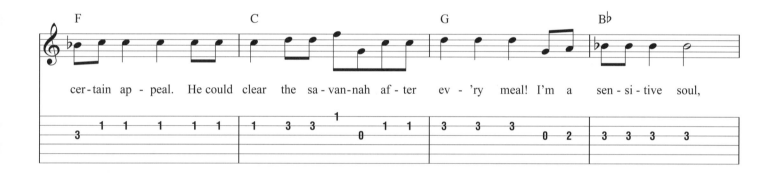

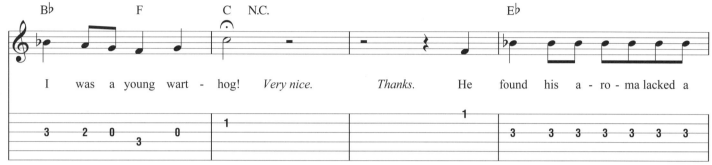

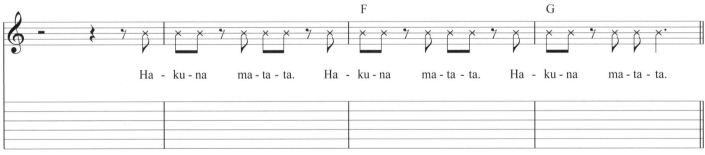

Happy Birthday to You

Words and Music by Mildred J. Hill and Patty S. Hill

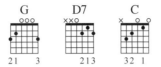

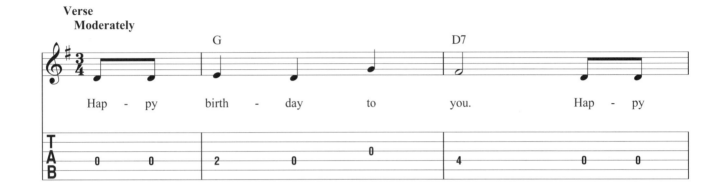

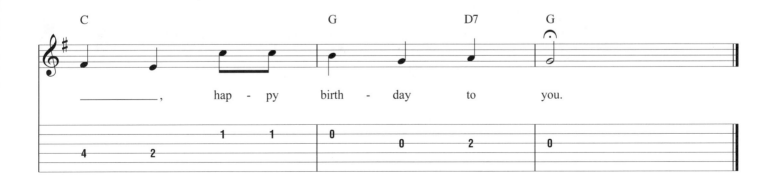

Happy Trails

from the Television Series THE ROY ROGERS SHOW
Words and Music by Dale Evans

If I Only Had a Brain

from THE WIZARD OF OZ

Lyric by E.Y. "Yip" Harburg
Music by Harold Arlen

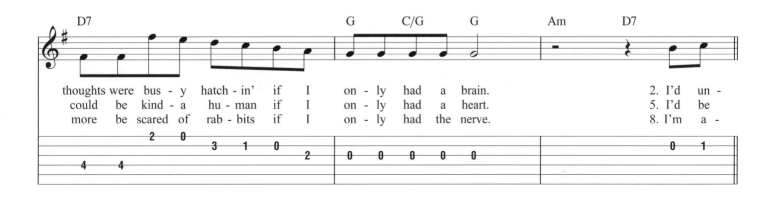

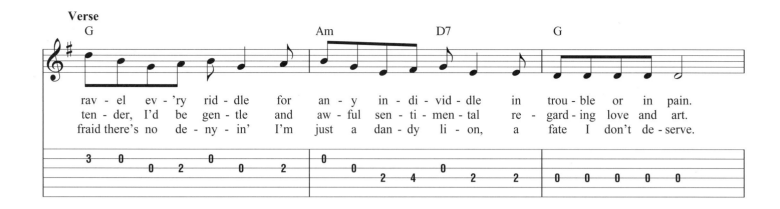

Verse

rav - el ev - 'ry rid - dle for an - y in - di - vid - dle in trou - ble or in pain.
ten - der, I'd be gen - tle and aw - ful sen - ti - men - tal re - gard - ing love and art.
fraid there's no de - ny - in' I'm just a dan - dy li - on, a fate I don't de - serve.

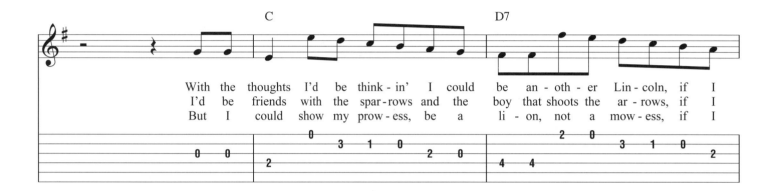

With the thoughts I'd be think - in' I could be an - oth - er Lin - coln, if I
I'd be friends with the spar - rows and the boy that shoots the ar - rows, if I
But I could show my prow - ess, be a li - on, not a mow - ess, if I

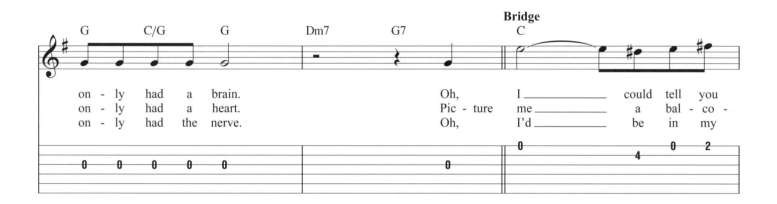

Bridge

on - ly had a brain. Oh, I _____ could tell you
on - ly had a heart. Pic - ture me _____ a bal - co -
on - ly had the nerve. Oh, I'd _____ be in my

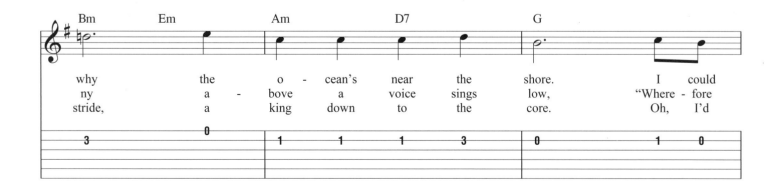

why the o - cean's near the shore. I could
ny a - bove a voice sings low, "Where - fore
stride, a king down to the core. Oh, I'd

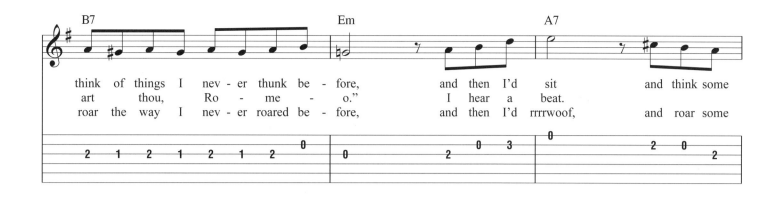

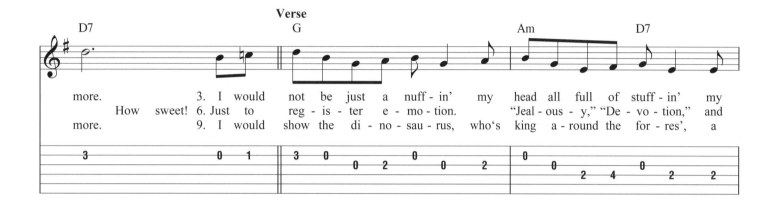

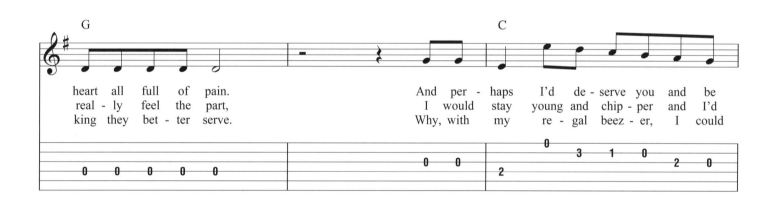

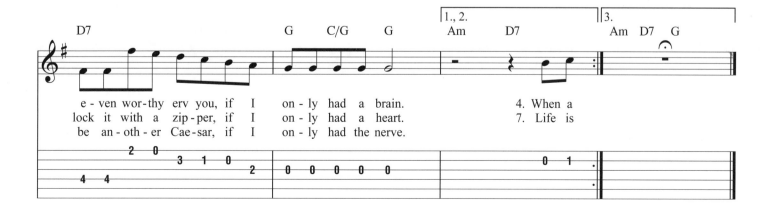

Heart and Soul

from the Paramount Short Subject A SONG IS BORN

Words by Frank Loesser
Music by Hoagy Carmichael

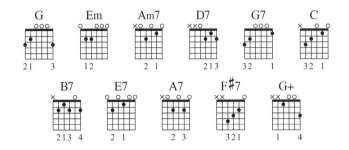

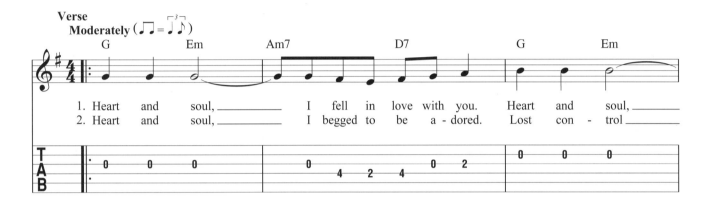

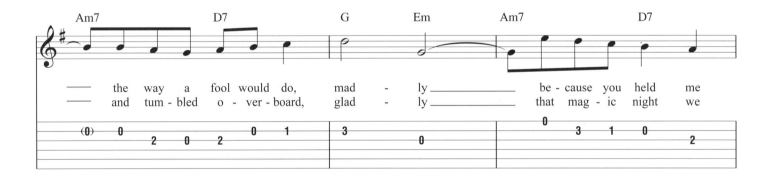

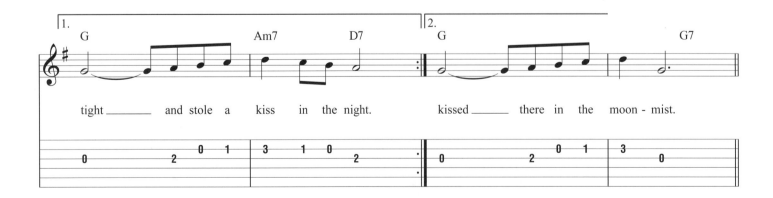

The Hokey Pokey

Words and Music by Charles P. Macak, Tafft Baker and Larry LaPrise

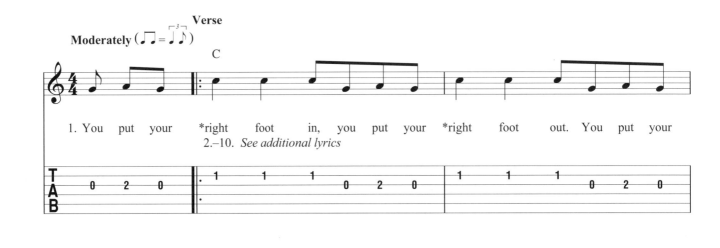

1. You put your *right foot in, you put your *right foot out. You put your
2.–10. *See additional lyrics*

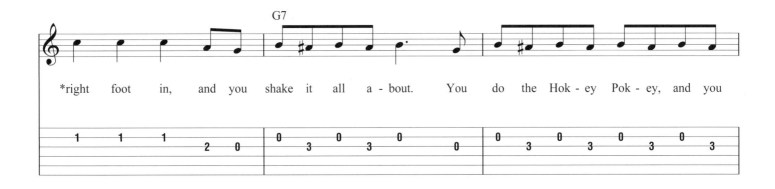

*right foot in, and you shake it all a - bout. You do the Hok - ey Pok - ey, and you

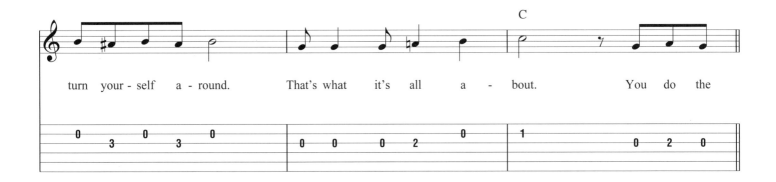

turn your - self a - round. That's what it's all a - bout. You do the

Chorus

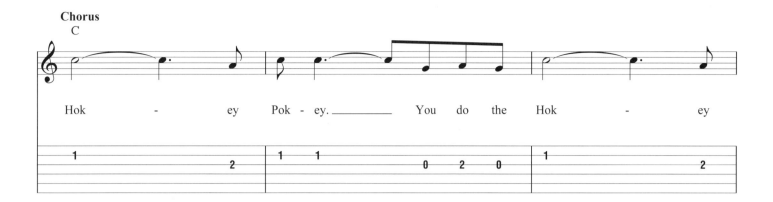

Hok - ey Pok - ey._____ You do the Hok - ey

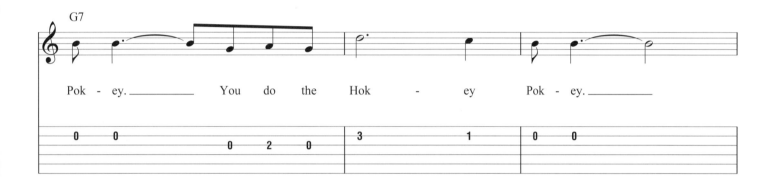

Pok - ey._____ You do the Hok - ey Pok - ey._____

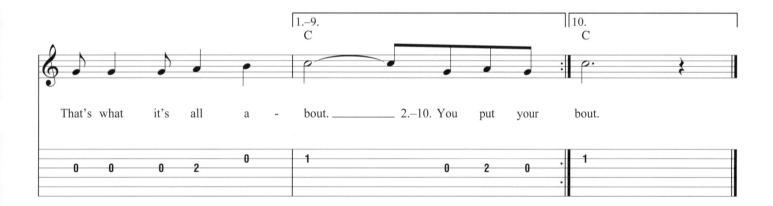

That's what it's all a - bout._____ 2.–10. You put your bout.

Additional Lyrics

*2nd time: left foot   *7th time: head
*3rd time: right arm   *8th time: right hip
*4th time: left arm   *9th time: left hip
*5th time: right elbow   *10th time: whole self
*6th time: left elbow

If You're Happy and You Know It

Words and Music by L. Smith

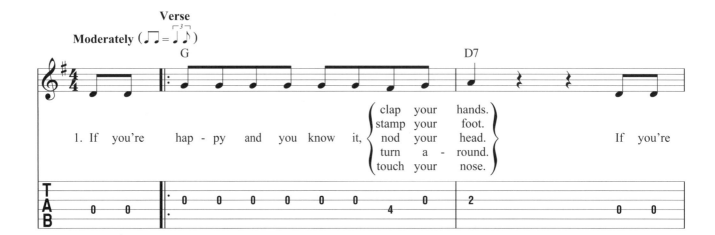

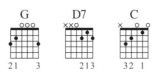

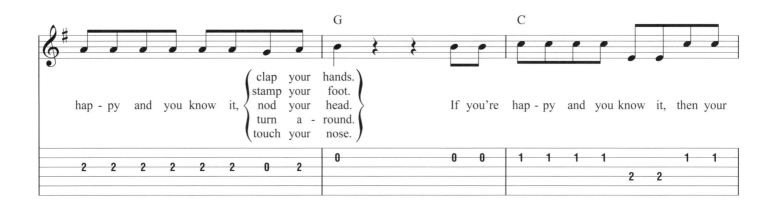

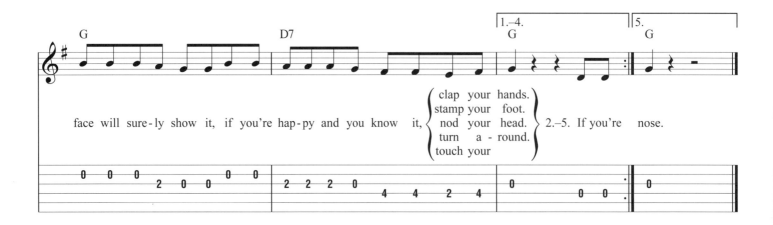

Kum Ba Yah

Traditional Spiritual

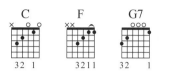

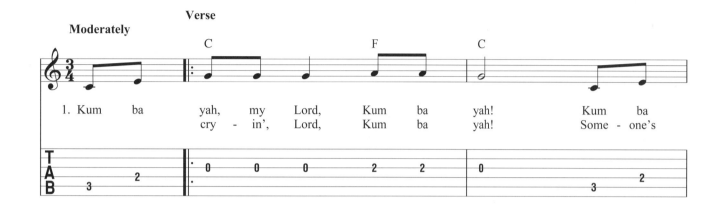

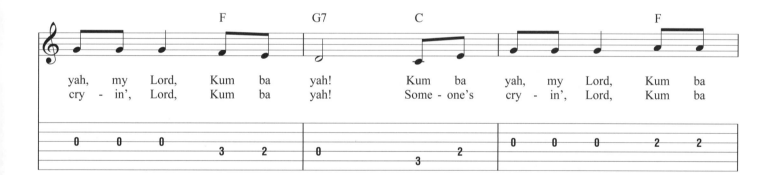

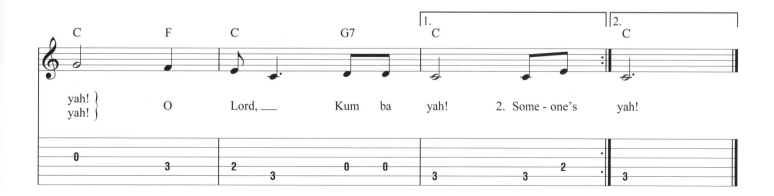

Let It Go
from FROZEN

Music and Lyrics by Kristen Anderson-Lopez and Robert Lopez

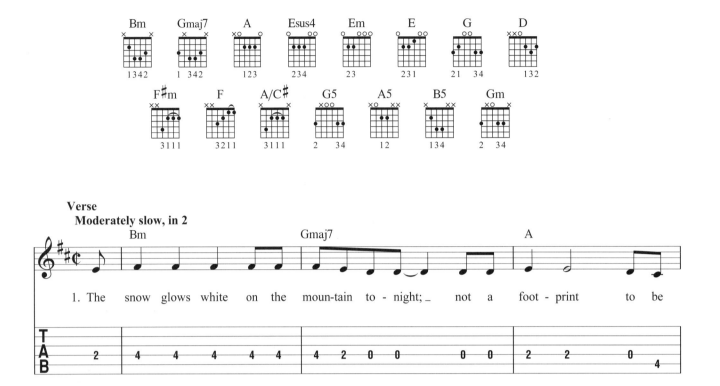

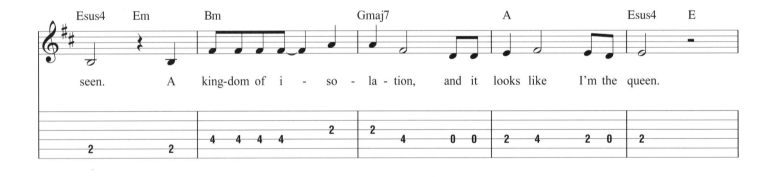

1. The snow glows white on the moun-tain to - night; _ not a foot - print to be

seen. A king-dom of i - so - la - tion, and it looks like I'm the queen.

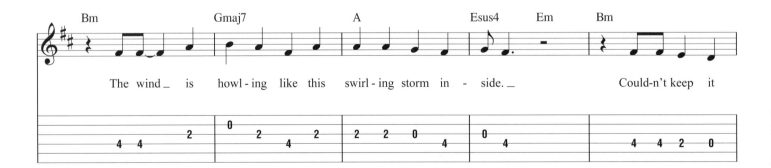

The wind _ is howl-ing like this swirl-ing storm in - side. _ Could-n't keep it

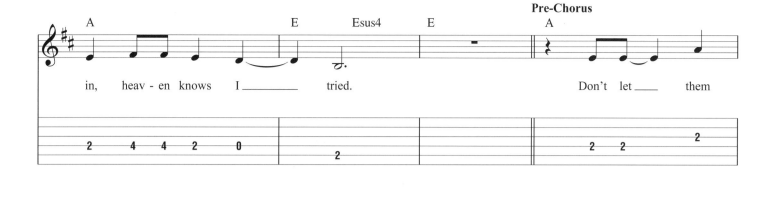

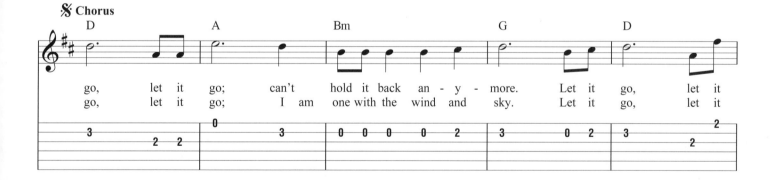

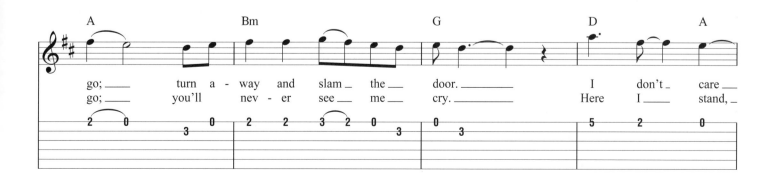

what they're go-ing to ___ say; ___ let the storm rage ___ on. ___
and here I'll ___ stay; ___ let the storm rage ___ on. ___

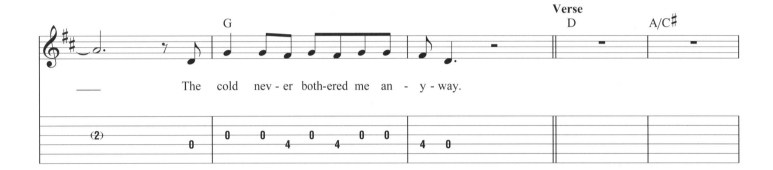

Verse

___ The cold nev-er both-ered me an-y-way.

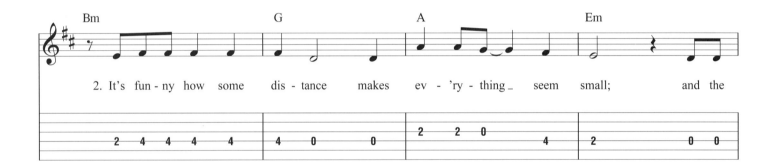

2. It's fun-ny how some dis-tance makes ev-'ry-thing ___ seem small; and the

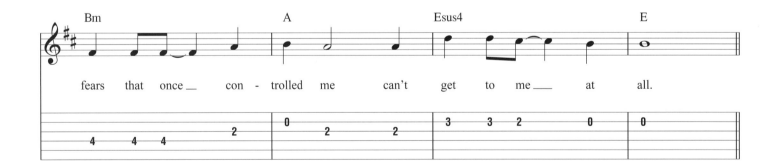

fears that once ___ con-trolled me can't get to me ___ at all.

Pre-Chorus

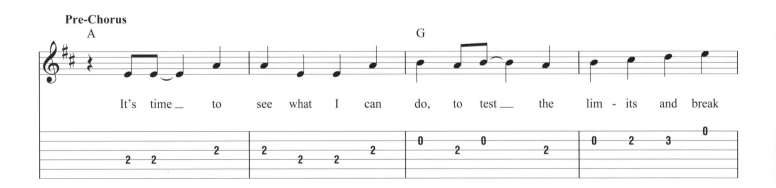

It's time ___ to see what I can do, to test ___ the lim-its and break

Coda

Bridge

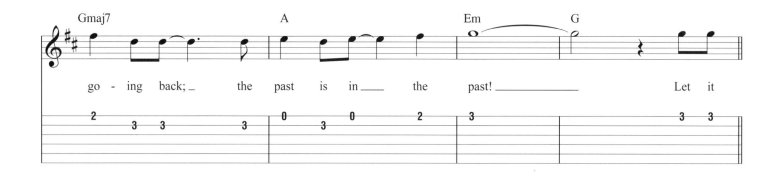

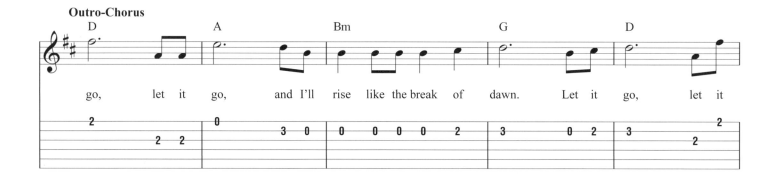

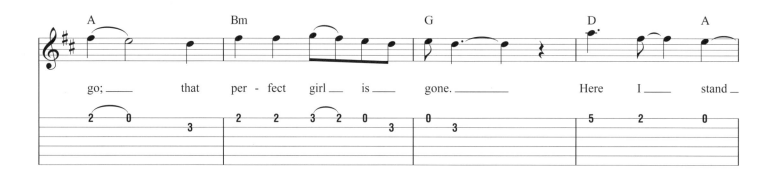

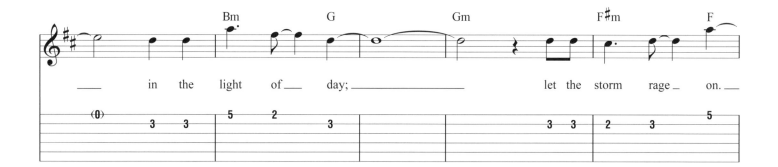

Little Brown Jug

Words and Music by Joseph E. Winner

Additional Lyrics

2. 'Tis you who makes my friends my foes,
   'Tis you who makes me wear old clothes.
   Here you are so near my nose,
   So tip her up and down she goes!

Linus and Lucy

from A CHARLIE BROWN CHRISTMAS

By Vince Guaraldi

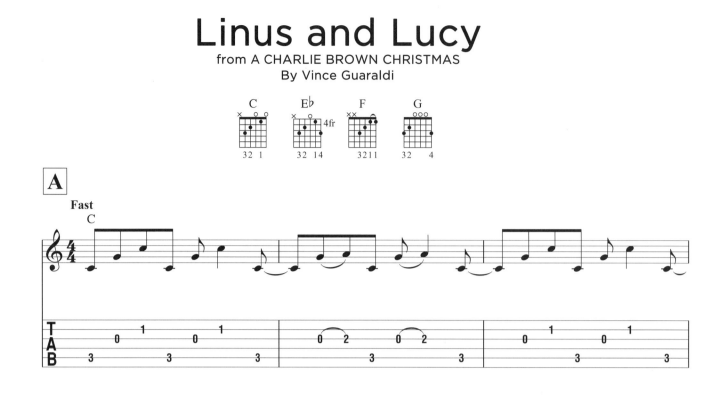

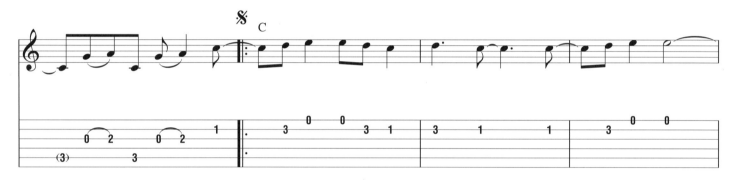

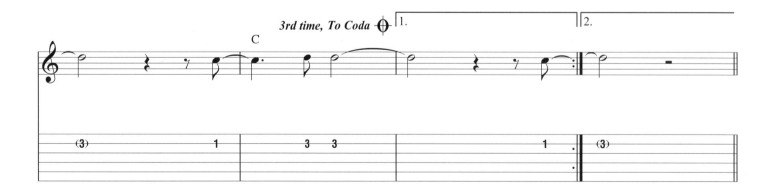

B

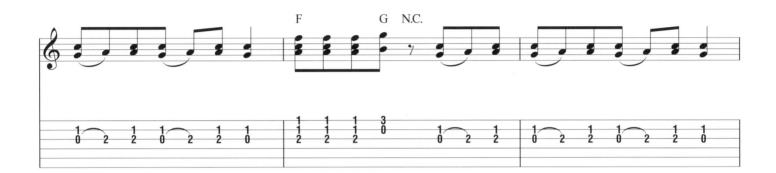

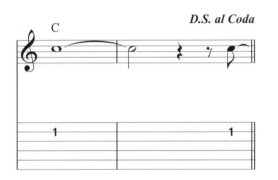

D.S. al Coda

⊕ **Coda**

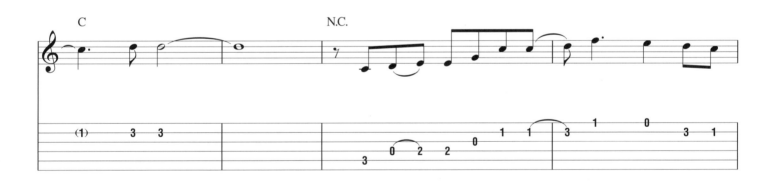

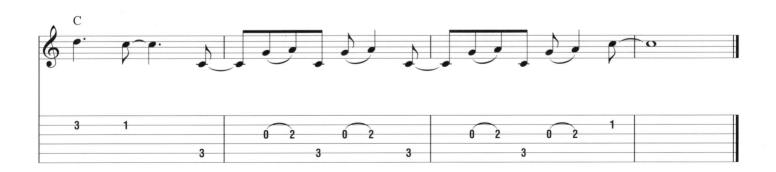

Little People

from LES MISÉRABLES

Music by Claude-Michel Schönberg
Lyrics by Alain Boublil, Jean-Marc Natel and Herbert Kretzme

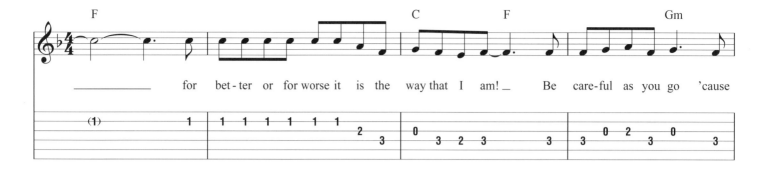

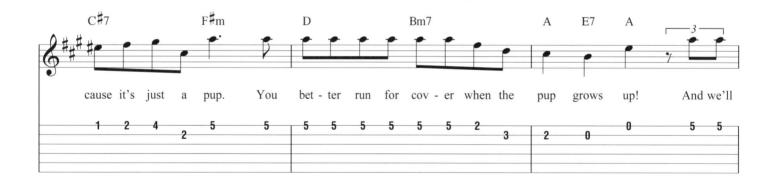

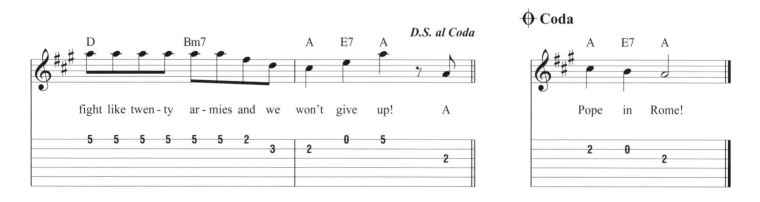

54

Octopus's Garden

Words and Music by Richard Starkey

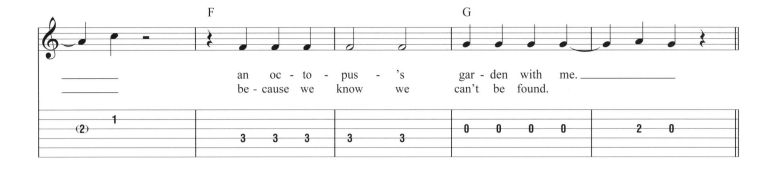

Chorus

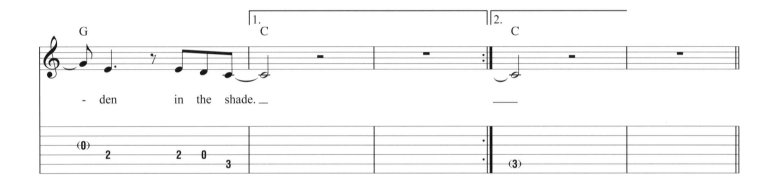

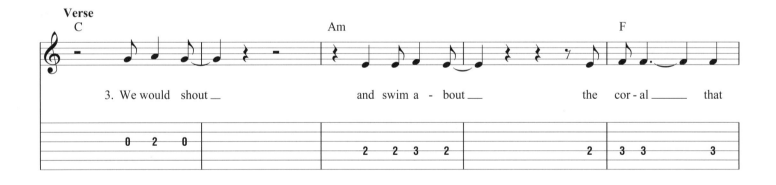

Verse

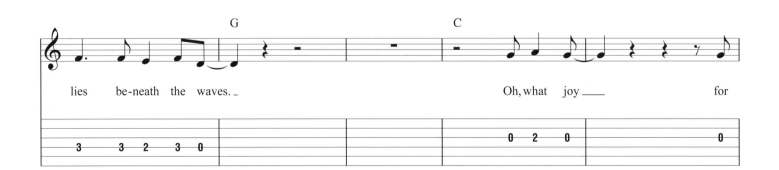

My Favorite Things

from THE SOUND OF MUSIC

Lyrics by Oscar Hammerstein II
Music by Richard Rodgers

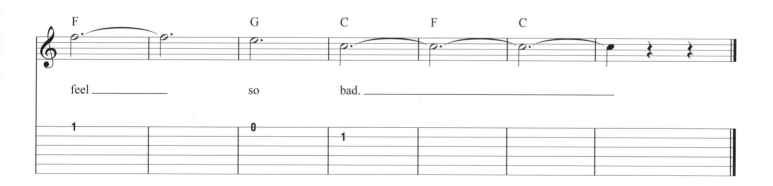

Additional Lyrics

2. Cream-colored ponies and crisp apple strudels,
   Doorbells and sleighbells and schnitzel with noodles,
   Wild geese that fly with the moon on their wings,
   These are a few of my favorite things.

On Top of Spaghetti

Words and Music by Tom Glazer

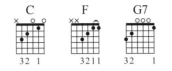

Verse

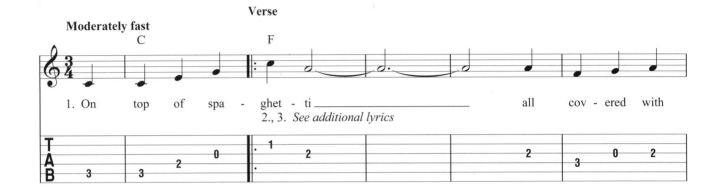

1. On top of spa - ghet - ti _____ all cov - ered with
2., 3. *See additional lyrics*

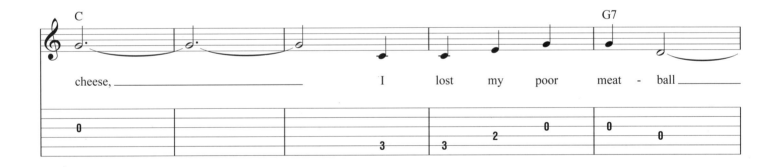

cheese, _____ I lost my poor meat - ball _____

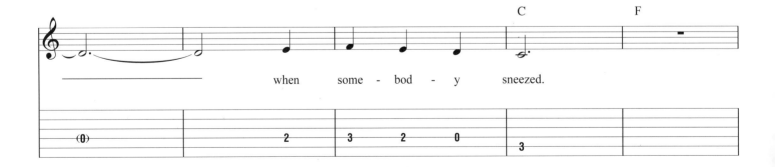

_____ when some - bod - y sneezed.

Additional Lyrics

2. It rolled in the garden and under a bush,
   And then my poor meatball was nothing but mush.
   The mush was as tasty as tasty could be,
   And early next summer, it grew into a tree.

3. The tree was all covered with beautiful moss;
   It grew lovely meatballs and tomato sauce.
   So if you eat spaghetti all covered with cheese,
   Hold onto your meatballs and don't ever sneeze.

Over the Rainbow

from THE WIZARD OF OZ

Music by Harold Arlen
Lyric by E.Y. "Yip" Harburg

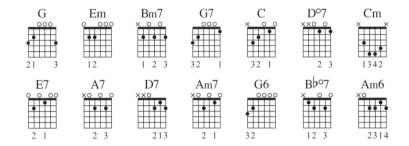

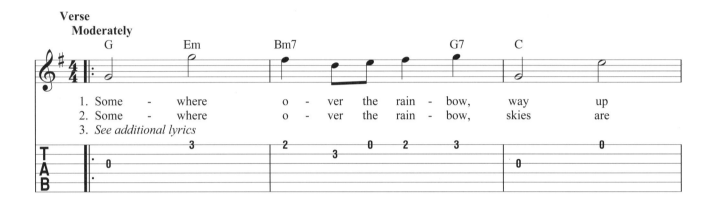

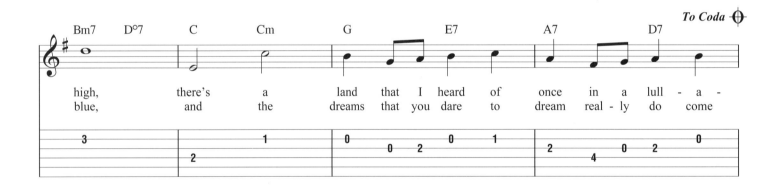

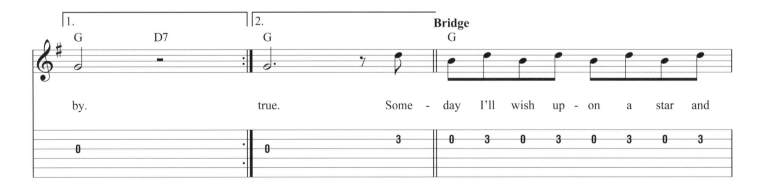

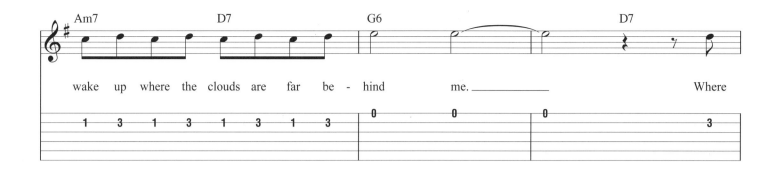

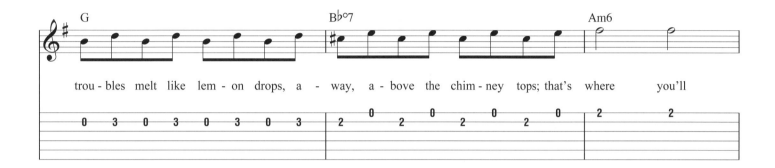

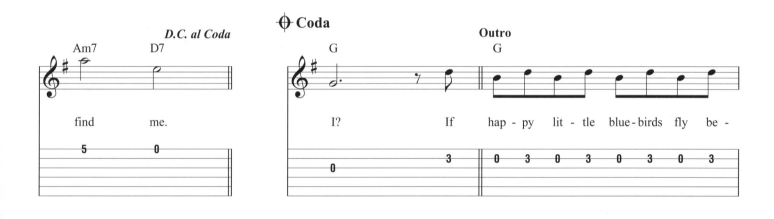

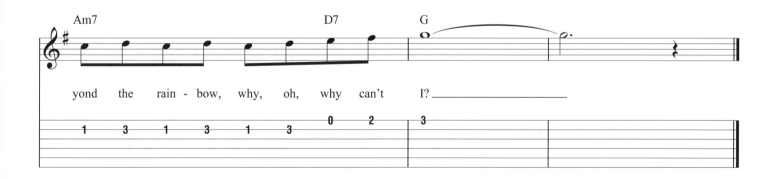

Additional Lyrics

3. Somewhere over the rainbow,
   Bluebirds fly.
   Birds fly over the rainbow,
   Why, then, oh, why can't I?

Puff the Magic Dragon

Words and Music by Lenny Lipton and Peter Yarrow

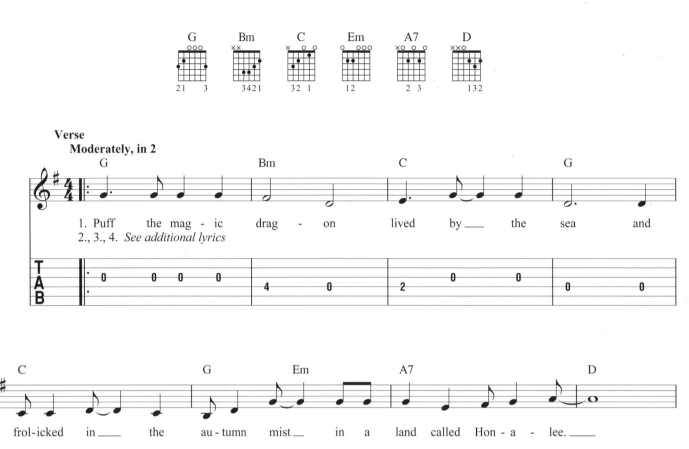

Verse
Moderately, in 2

1. Puff the mag - ic drag - on lived by ___ the sea and
2., 3., 4. *See additional lyrics*

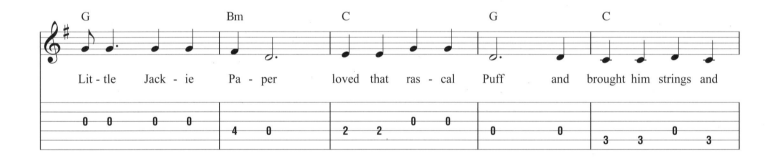

frol-icked in ___ the au - tumn mist ___ in a land called Hon - a - lee. ___

Lit - tle Jack - ie Pa - per loved that ras - cal Puff and brought him strings and

seal-ing wax ___ and oth - er fan - cy stuff. Oh! Puff the mag - ic drag - on

Additional Lyrics

2. Together they would travel on a boat with billowed sail.
Jackie kept a lookout perched on Puff's gigantic tail.
Noble kings and princes would bow whene'er they came.
Pirate ships would low'r their flag when Puff roared out his name. Oh!

3. A dragon lives forever, but not so little boys.
Painted wings and giant rings make way for other toys.
One gray night it happened, Jackie Paper came no more,
And Puff that mighty dragon, he ceased his fearless roar. Oh!

4. His head was bent in sorrow, green tears fell like rain.
Puff no longer went to play along the Cherry Lane.
Without his lifelong friend, Puff could not be brave,
So Puff that mighty dragon sadly slipped into his cave. Oh!

The Rainbow Connection

from THE MUPPET MOVIE

Words and Music by Paul Williams and Kenneth L. Ascher

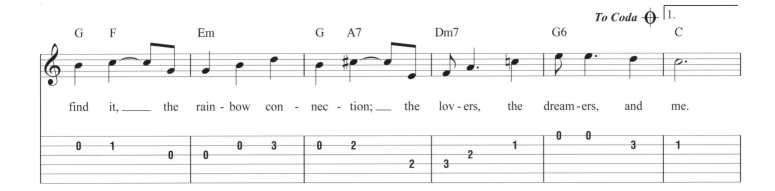

find it, _____ the rain - bow con - nec - tion; ___ the lov - ers, the dream - ers, and me.

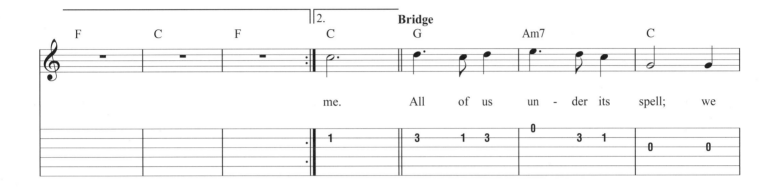

me.   All   of   us   un - der   its   spell;   we

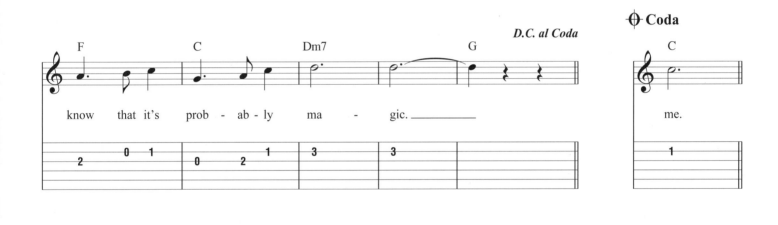

know   that   it's   prob - ab - ly   ma - gic. _____   me.

La,   da,   da,   dee,   da,   da,   do.   La,   la,   da,   da,   da,   de,   da,   do. _____

Additional Lyrics

2. Who said that ev'ry wish could be heard and answered
When wished on the morning star?
Somebody thought of that, and someone believed it;
Look what it's done so far.

3. Have you been half asleep and have you heard voices?
I've heard them calling my name.
Is this the sweet sound that calls the young sailors?
The voice might be one and the same.

Sesame Street Theme

from the Television Series SESAME STREET
Words by Bruce Hart, Jon Stone and Joe Raposo
Music by Joe Raposo

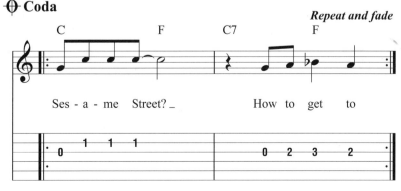

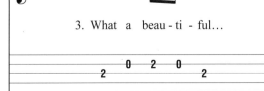

Sing

from SESAME STREET
Words and Music by Joe Raposo

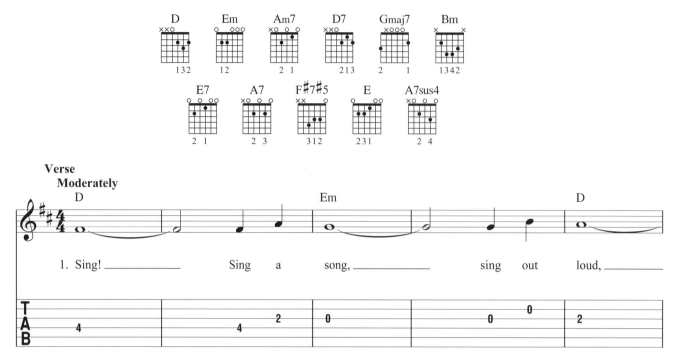

Verse
Moderately

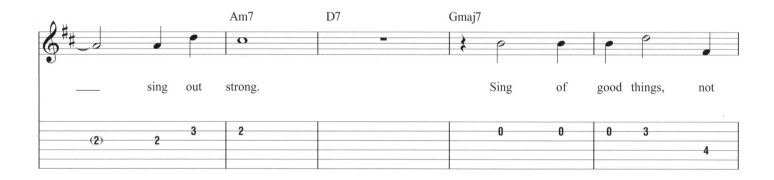

1. Sing! _____ Sing a song, _____ sing out loud, _____

_____ sing out strong. Sing of good things, not

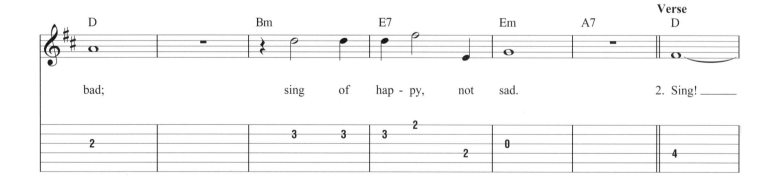

bad; sing of hap-py, not sad. 2. Sing! _____

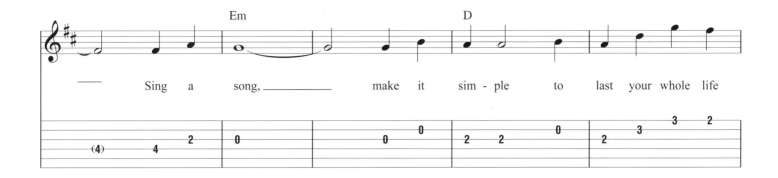

Sing a song, _____ make it sim - ple to last your whole life

long. _____ Don't wor - ry that it's not good e - nough for an - y - one else to

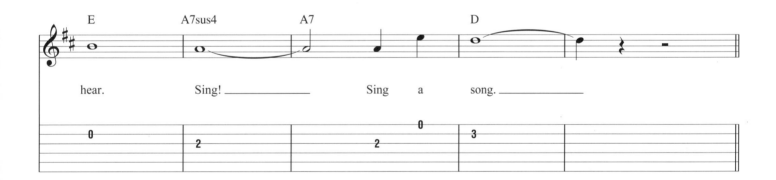

hear. Sing! _____ Sing a song. _____

Outro

Repeat and fade

La, la do, la, da. La, da, la, do la, da. La, da, da, la, do, la, da. _____

Singin' in the Rain

from SINGIN' IN THE RAIN

Lyric by Arthur Freed
Music by Nacio Herb Brown

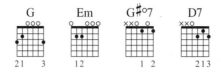

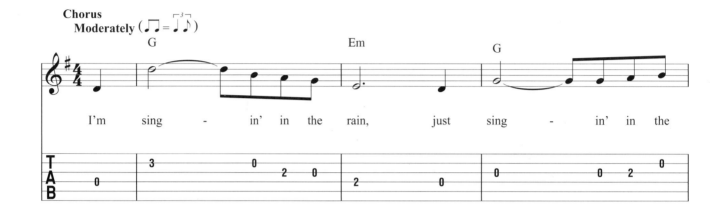

I'm sing - in' in the rain, just sing - in' in the

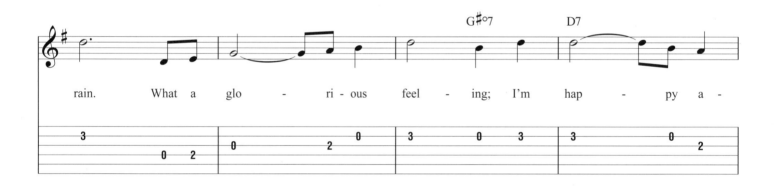

rain. What a glo - ri - ous feel - ing; I'm hap - py a -

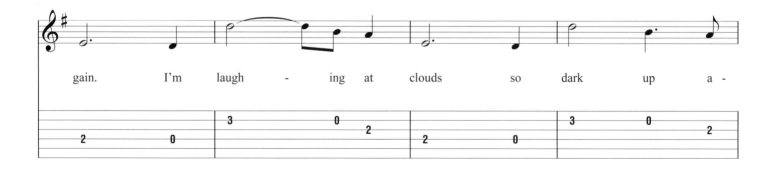

gain. I'm laugh - ing at clouds so dark up a -

All Rights Controlled and Administered by EMI ROBBINS CATALOG INC. (Publishing) and ALFRED MUSIC (Print)
All Rights Reserved   Used by Permission

Skating

By Vince Guaraldi

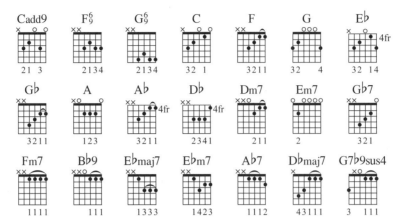

Intro
Fast, in 1

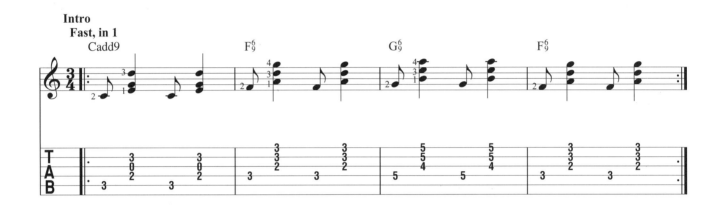

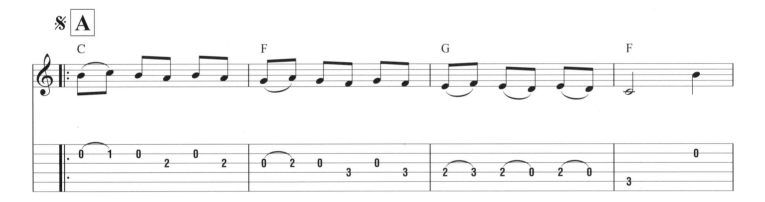

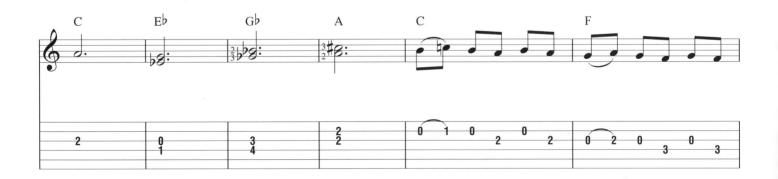

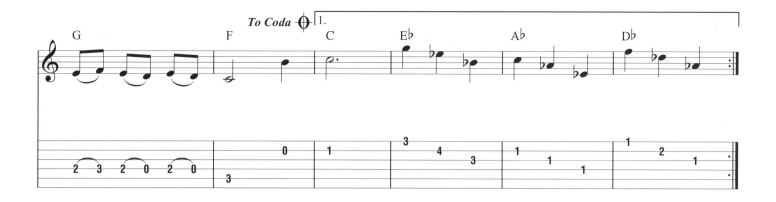

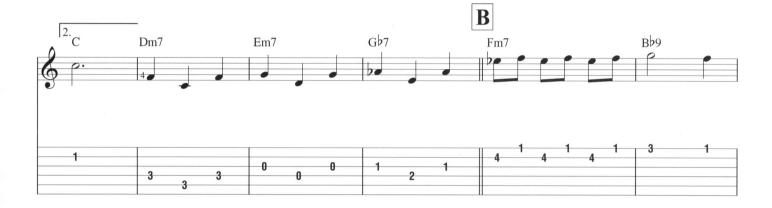

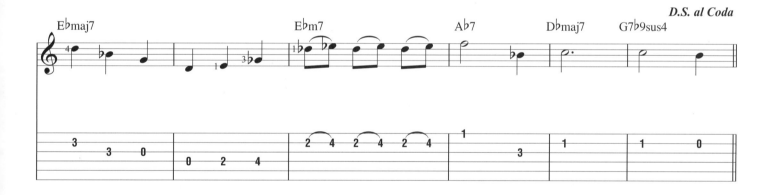

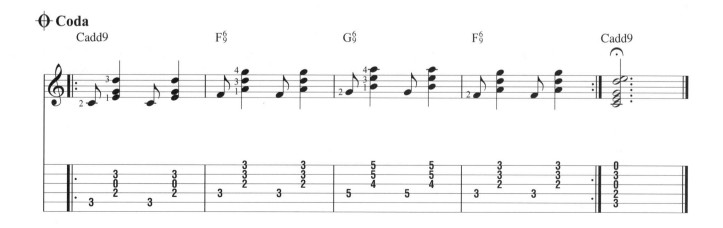

Splish Splash

Words and Music by Bobby Darin and Murray Kaufman

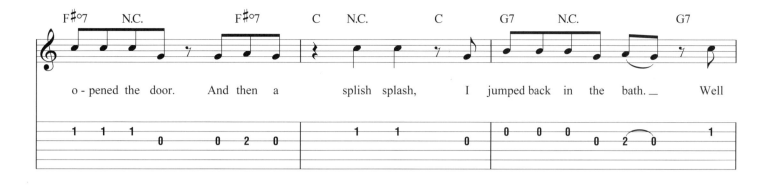

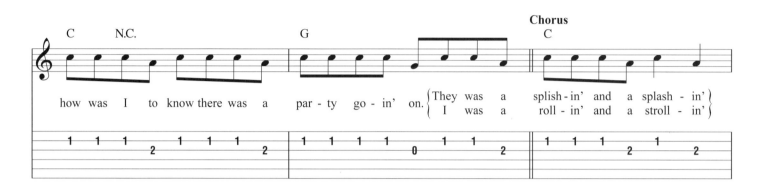

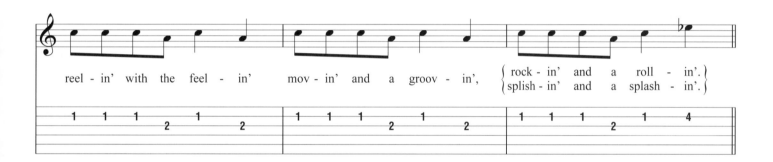

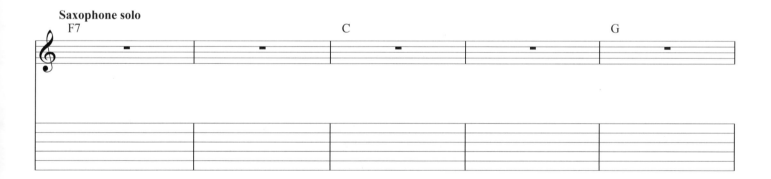

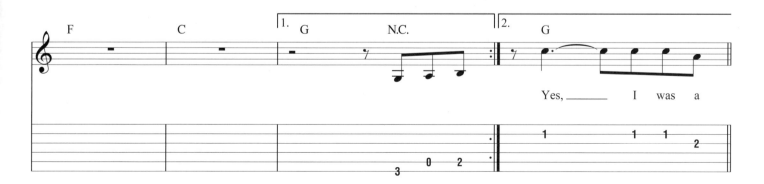

Chorus

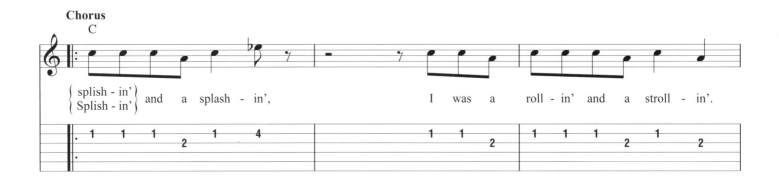

Repeat and fade

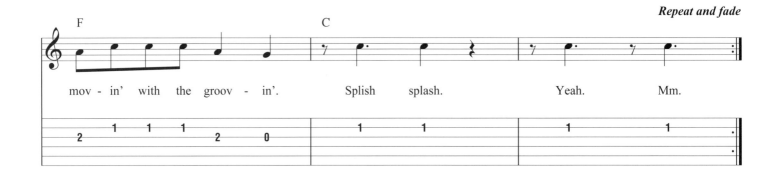

Additional Lyrics

2. Bing bang, I saw the whole gang
Dancin' on my livin' room rug. Yeah!
Flip flop, they was doin' the bop,
All the teens had the dancin' bug.
There was Lollipop a with a Peggy Sue.
Good golly, Miss Molly was a even there too.
A well a splish splash, I forgot about the bath.
I went and put my dancin' shoes on, yeah.

SpongeBob SquarePants Theme Song

from SPONGEBOB SQUAREPANTS

Words and Music by Mark Harrison, Blaise Smith, Steve Hillenburg and Derek Drymon

*Lyrics in italics are shouted throughout.

The Star-Spangled Banner

Words by Francis Scott Key
Music by John Stafford Smith

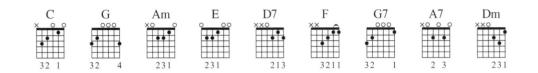

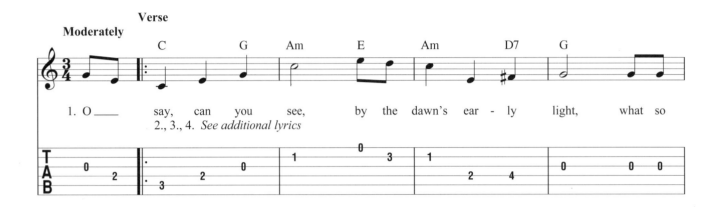

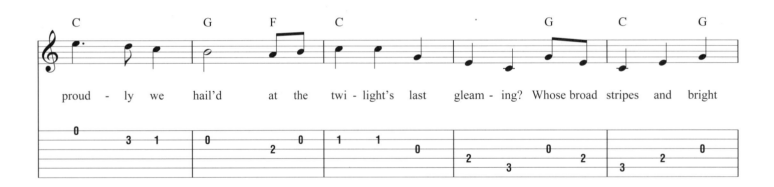

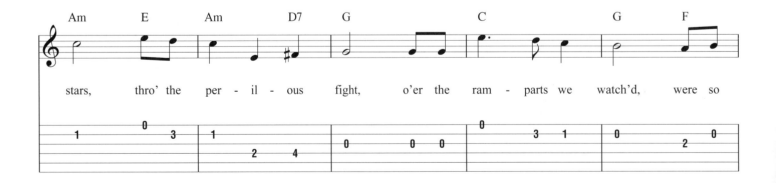

Additional Lyrics

2. On the shore dimly seen thro' the mists of the deep,
   Where the foe's haughty host in dread silence reposes,
   What is that which the breeze, o'er the towering steep,
   As it fitfully blows, half conceals, half discloses?
   Now it catches the gleam of the morning's first beam,
   In full glory reflected now shines in the stream.
   'Tis the star-spangled banner, o long may it wave
   O'er the land of the free and the home of the brave.

3. And where is the band who so dauntingly swore,
   'Mid the havoc of war and the battle's confusion.
   A home and a country they'd leave us no more?
   Their blood has wash'd out their foul footstep's pollution.
   No refuge could save the hireling and slave
   From the terror of flight or the gloom of the grave.
   And the star-spangled banner in triumph doth wave
   O'er the land of the free and the home of the brave.

4. O thus be it ever when free man shall stand,
   Between their loved homes and the war's desolation.
   Blest with the vic'try and peace, may the heav'n rescued land
   Praise the Power that hath made and preserved us a nation!
   Then conquer we must when our cause it is just,
   And this be our motto, "In God is our trust!"
   And the star-spangled banner in triumph shall wave
   O'er the land of the free and the home of the brave.

Supercalifragilisticexpialidocious

from MARY POPPINS

Words and Music by Richard M. Sherman and Robert B. Sherman

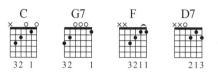

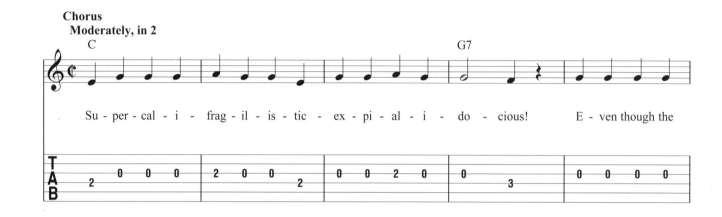

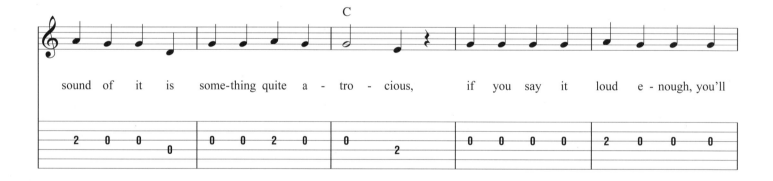

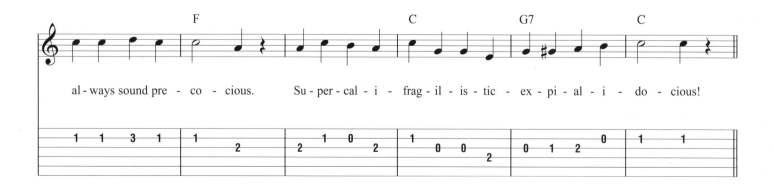

Interlude

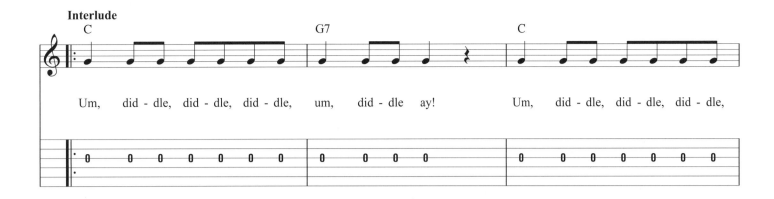

Um, did - dle, did - dle, did - dle, um, did - dle ay! Um, did - dle, did - dle, did - dle,

Verse

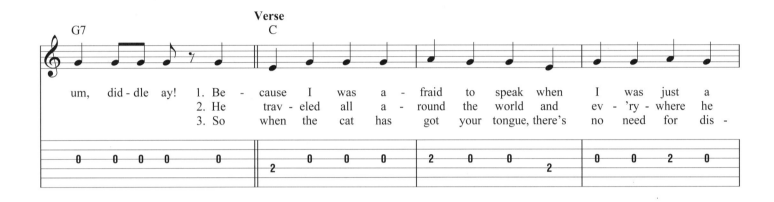

um, did - dle ay!
1. Be - cause I was a - fraid to speak when I was just a
2. He trav - eled all a - round the world and ev - 'ry - where he
3. So when the cat has got your tongue, there's no need for dis -

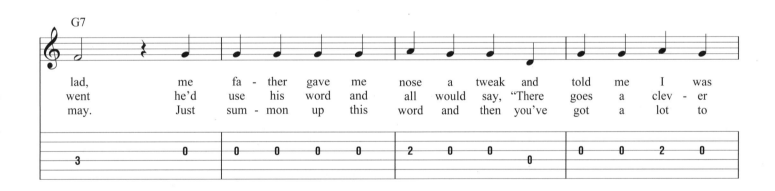

lad, me fa - ther gave me nose a tweak and told me I was
went he'd use his word and all would say, "There goes a clev - er
may. Just sum - mon up this word and then you've got a lot to

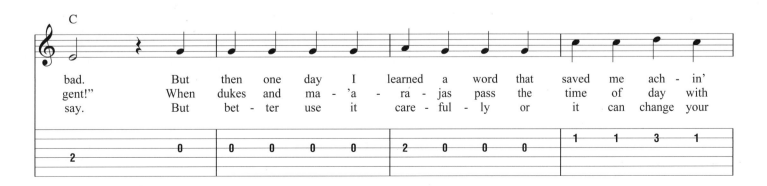

bad. But then one day I learned a word that saved me ach - in'
gent!" When dukes and ma - 'a - ra - jas pass the time of day with
say. But bet - ter use it care - ful - ly or it can change your

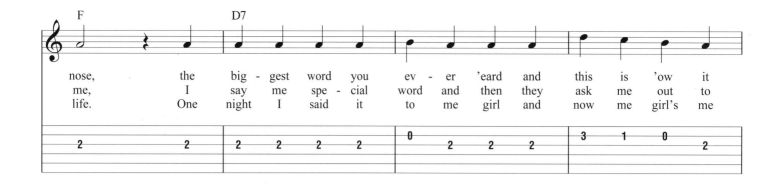

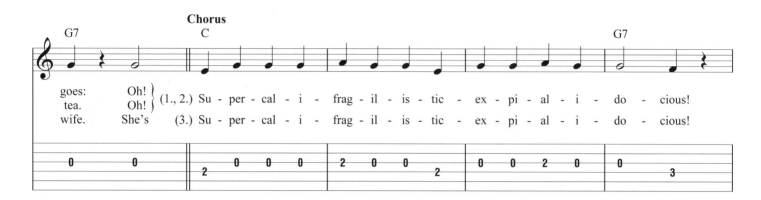

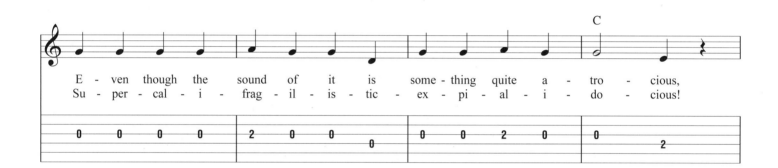

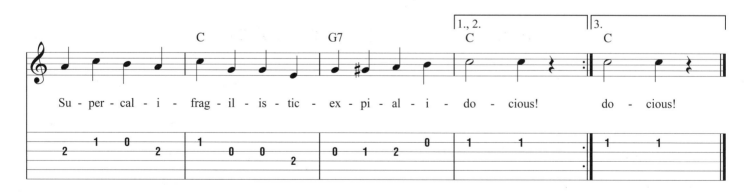

Take Me Out to the Ball Game

Words by Jack Norworth
Music by Albert von Tilzer

This Land Is Your Land

Words and Music by Woody Guthrie

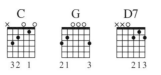

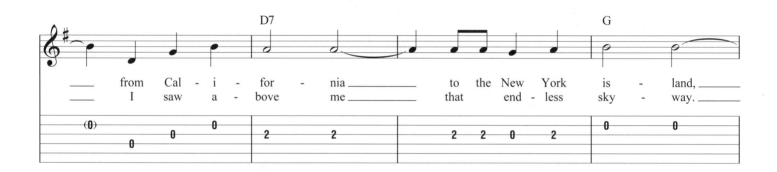

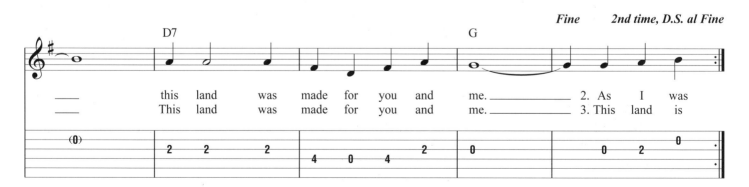

This Old Man

Traditional

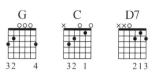

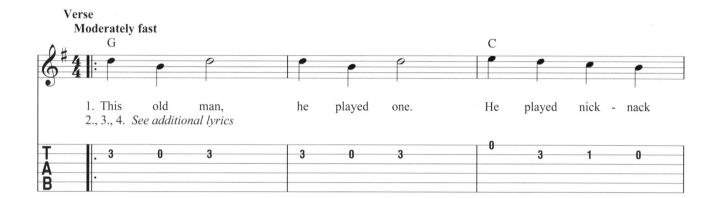

Verse
Moderately fast

1. This old man, he played one. He played nick-nack
2., 3., 4. *See additional lyrics*

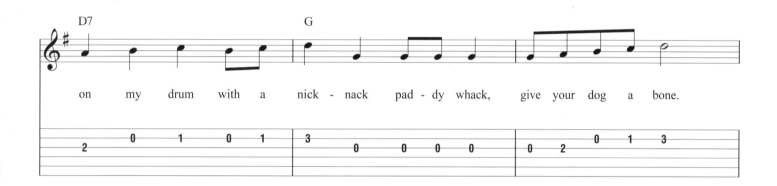

on my drum with a nick-nack pad-dy whack, give your dog a bone.

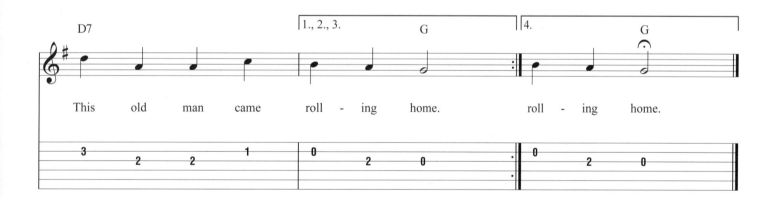

This old man came roll-ing home. roll-ing home.

Additional Lyrics

2. This old man, he played two.
   He played nicknack on my shoe with a
   Nicknack paddy whack, give your dog a bone.
   This old man came rolling home.

3. This old man, he played three.
   He played nicknack on my knee with a
   Nicknack paddy whack, give your dog a bone.
   This old man came rolling home.

4. This old man, he played four.
   He played nicknack on my door with a
   Nicknack paddy whack, give your dog a bone.
   This old man came rolling home.

Tomorrow

from the Musical Production ANNIE

Lyric by Martin Charnin
Music by Charles Strouse

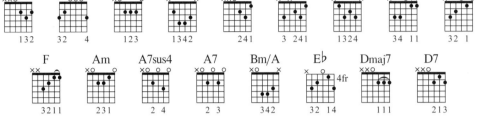

Verse

Slowly, in 2

1. The sun - 'll come out _____ to - mor - row. _____ Bet your bot - tom
think - in' a - bout _____ to - mor - row _____ clears a - way the

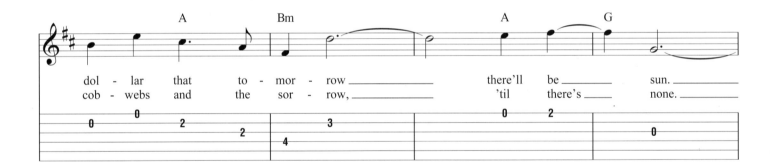

dol - lar that to - mor - row _____ there'll be _____ sun. _____
cob - webs and the sor - row, _____ 'til there's _____ none. _____

2. Just _____ When I'm stuck with a day that's gray and

lone - ly,   I   just   stick   out   my   chin   and   grin,   and   say: _____

Outro

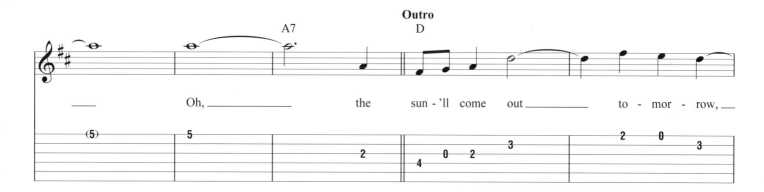

_____ Oh, _____ the   sun - 'll   come   out _____ to - mor - row, _____

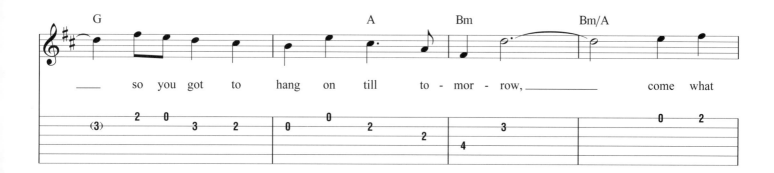

_____ so   you   got   to   hang   on   till   to - mor - row, _____ come   what

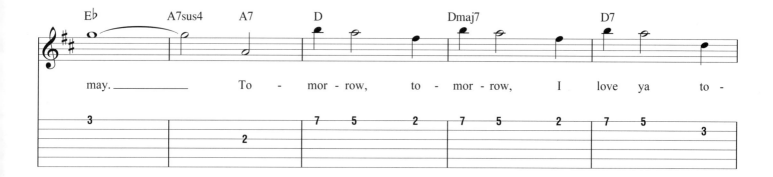

may. _____ To - mor - row,   to - mor - row,   I   love   ya   to -

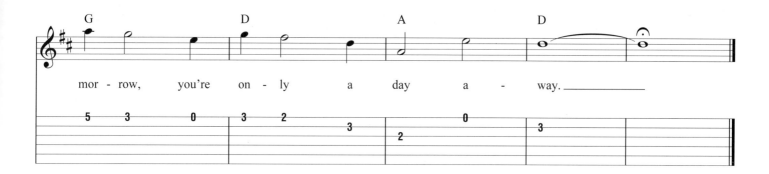

mor - row,   you're   on - ly   a   day   a - way. _____

The Unicorn

Words and Music by Shel Silverstein

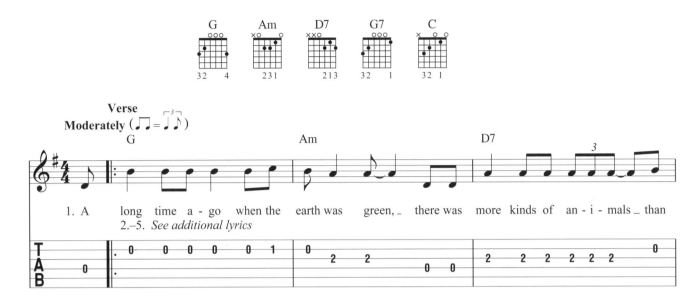

Verse
Moderately

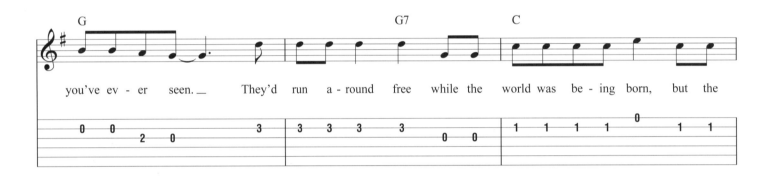

1. A long time a-go when the earth was green,_ there was more kinds of an-i-mals_ than
2.–5. *See additional lyrics*

you've ev-er seen._ They'd run a-round free while the world was be-ing born, but the

Chorus

love-li-est of all was the u-ni-corn. There was green al-li-ga-tors and

long-necked geese,_ some hump-ty-backed cam-els and some chim-pan-zees,_ some

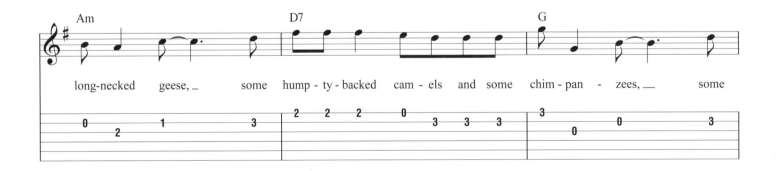

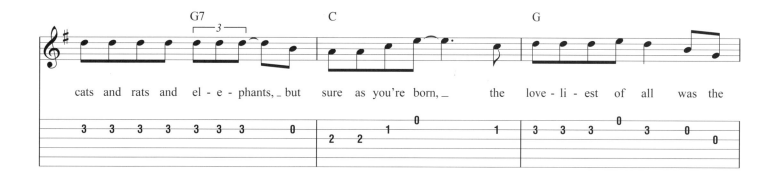

cats and rats and el - e - phants, but sure as you're born, the love - li - est of all was the

un - i - corn.

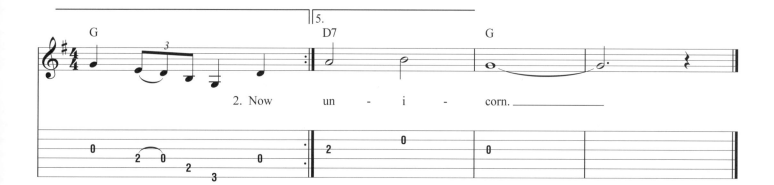

2. Now un - i - corn.

Additional Lyrics

2. Now God seen some sinnin' and it gave Him pain
And He says, "Stand back, I'm going to make it rain."
He says, "Hey, brother Noah, I'll tell you what to do,"
Build me a floating zoo."

Chorus 2. "And take some of them green alligators and long-necked geese,
Some humpty-backed camels and some chimpanzees,
Some cats and rats and elephants, but sure as you're born
Don't forget my unicorn."

3. Old Noah was there to answer the call.
He finished up making the ark just as the rain started fallin',
He marched in the animals two by two,
And he called out as they went through:

Chorus 3. "Hey, Lord, I've got your green alligators and long-necked geese,
Some humpty-backed camels and some chimpanzees,
Some cats and rats and elephants, but Lord, I'm so forlorn
I just can't see no unicorn."

4. Then Noah looked out through the drivin' rain,
Them unicorns were hiding, playin' silly games,
Kickin' and splashin' while the rain was pourin'.
Oh, them silly unicorns.

Chorus 4. There was green alligators and long-necked geese,
Some humpty-backed camels and some chimpanzees,
Noah cried, "Close the door 'cause the rain is pourin'.
And we just can't wait for no unicorns."

5. The ark started movin'; it drifted with the tide.
Them unicorns looked up from the rocks and they cried,
And the waters came down and sort of floated them away,

Spoken: *And that's why you never seen a unicorn, to this very day.*

Chorus 5. You'll see green alligators and long-necked geese,
Some humpty-backed camels and come chimpanzees,
Some cats and rats and elephants, but sure as you're born,
You're never gonna see no unicorn.

When I Grow Too Old to Dream

Lyrics by Oscar Hammerstein II
Music by Sigmund Romberg

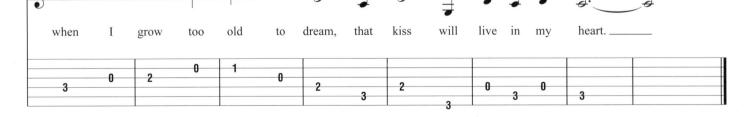

Yankee Doodle

Traditional

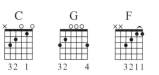

Verse
Moderately

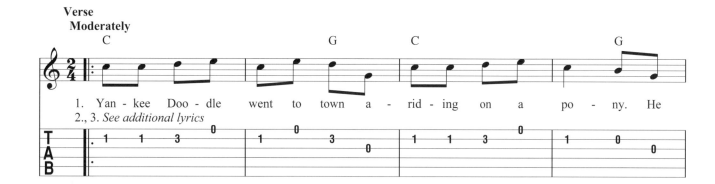

1. Yan - kee Doo - dle went to town a - rid - ing on a po - ny. He
2., 3. *See additional lyrics*

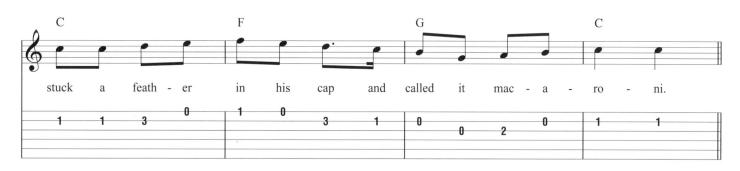

stuck a feath - er in his cap and called it mac - a - ro - ni.

Chorus

Yan - kee Doo - dle keep it up. Yan - kee Doo - dle dan - dy. Mind the mu - sic

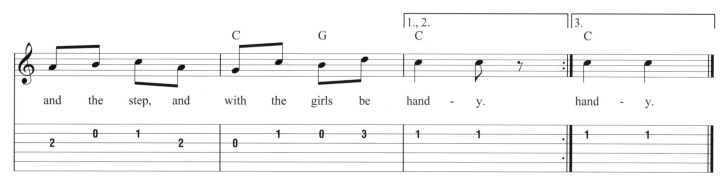

and the step, and with the girls be hand - y. hand - y.

Additional Lyrics

2. Fath'r and I went down to camp
Along with Captain Goodwin
And there we saw the men and boys
As thick as hasty puddin'.

3. And there was Captain Washington
Upon a slapping stallion
A-giving orders to his men,
I guess there was a million.

Won't You Be My Neighbor?
(It's a Beautiful Day in the Neighborhood)

from MISTER ROGERS' NEIGHBORHOOD
Words and Music by Fred Rogers

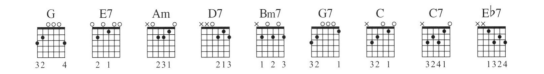

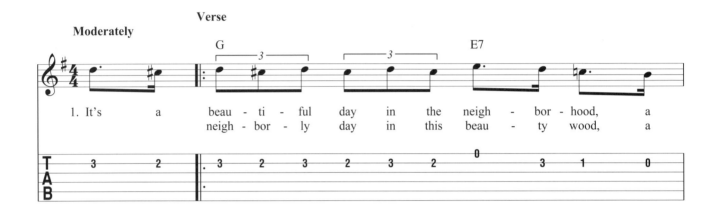

Verse

Moderately

1. It's a beau - ti - ful day in the neigh - bor - hood, a
neigh - bor - ly day in this beau - ty wood, a

beau - ti - ful day for a neigh - bor. Would you be mine? _____ Could you
neigh - bor - ly day for a beau - ty. Would you be mine? _____ Could you

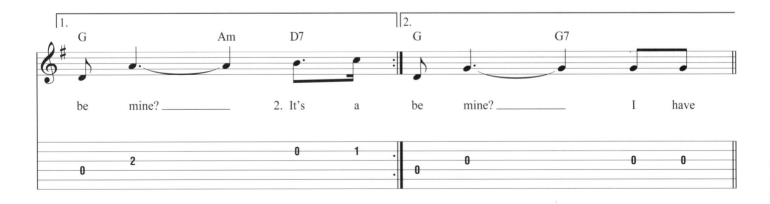

be mine? _____ 2. It's a be mine? _____ I have

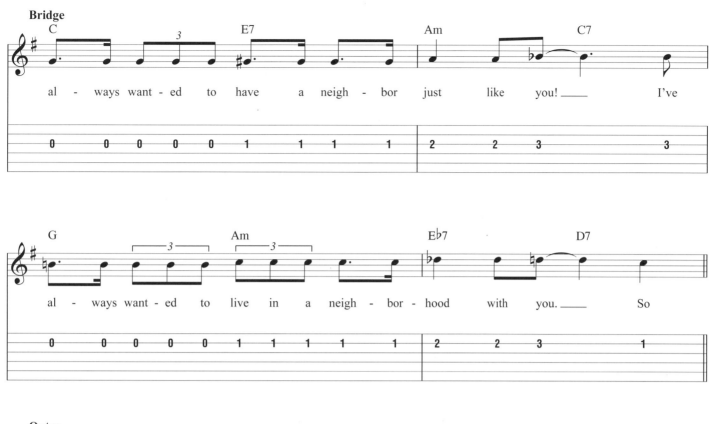

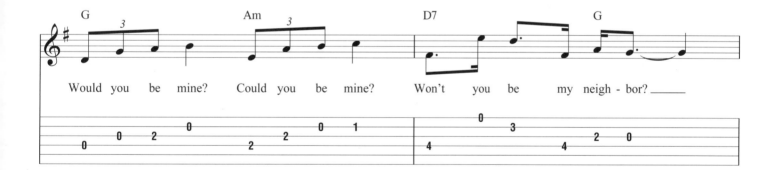

You Are My Sunshine

Words and Music by Jimmie Davis

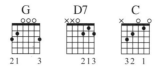

Verse

Moderately, in 2

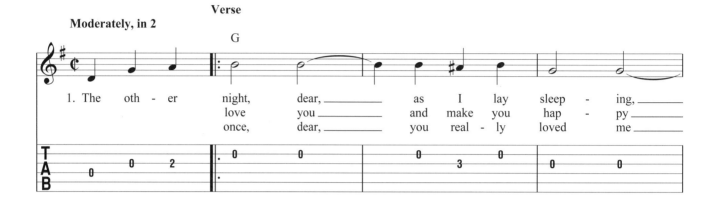

1. The oth - er night, dear, _____ as I lay sleep - ing, _____
   love you _____ and make you hap - py _____
   once, dear, _____ you real - ly loved me _____

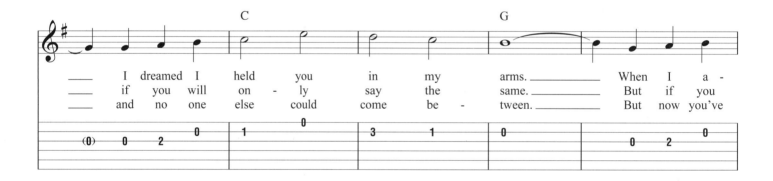

_____ I dreamed I held you in my arms. _____ When I a -
_____ if you will on - ly say the same. _____ But if you
_____ and no one else could come be - tween. _____ But now you've

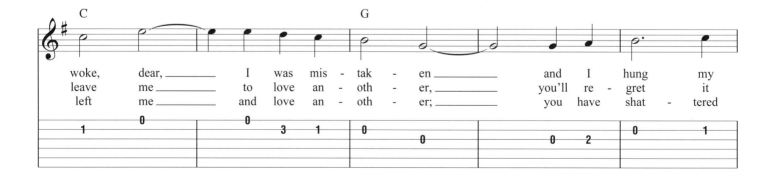

woke, dear, _____ I was mis - tak - en _____ and I hung my
leave me _____ to love an - oth - er, _____ you'll re - gret it
left me _____ and love an - oth - er; _____ you have shat - tered

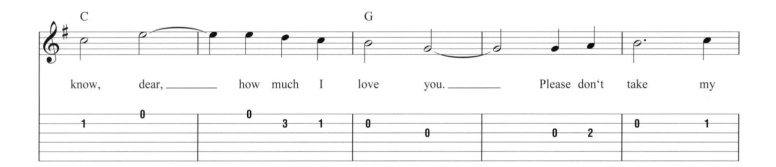

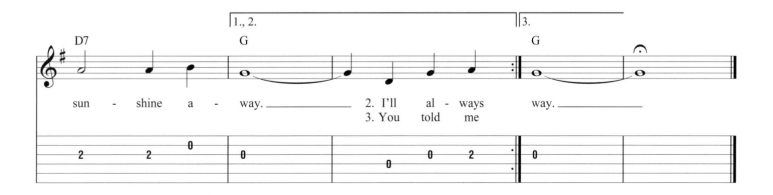

Zip-A-Dee-Doo-Dah

from SONG OF THE SOUTH
from Disneyland and Walt Disney World's SPLASH MOUNTAIN

Music by Allie Wrubel
Words by Ray Gilbert

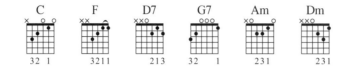

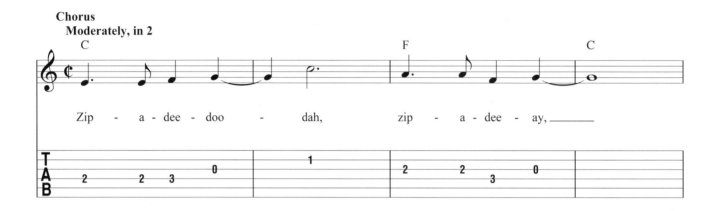

Chorus
Moderately, in 2

Zip - a - dee - doo - dah, zip - a - dee - ay, _____

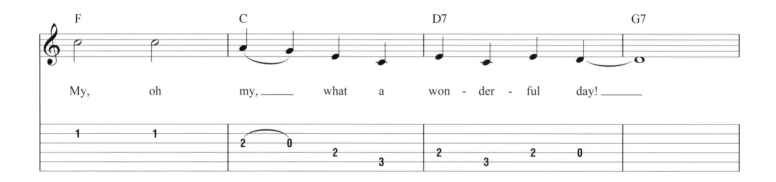

My, oh my, _____ what a won - der - ful day! _____

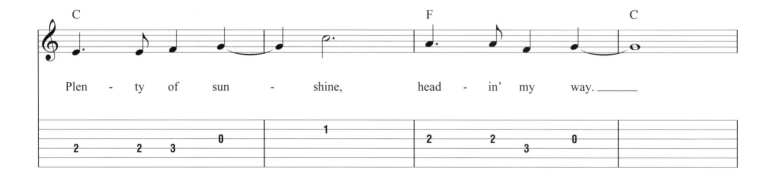

Plen - ty of sun - shine, head - in' my way. _____

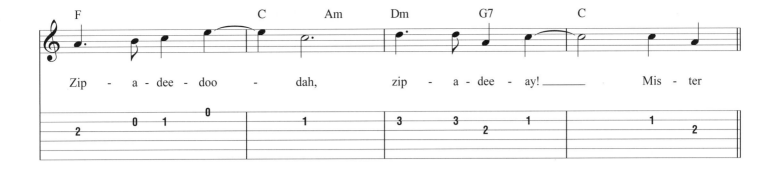

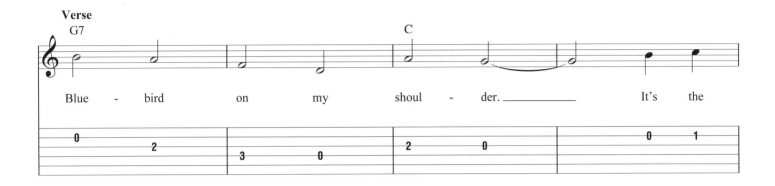

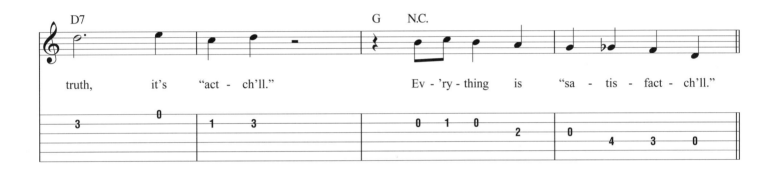

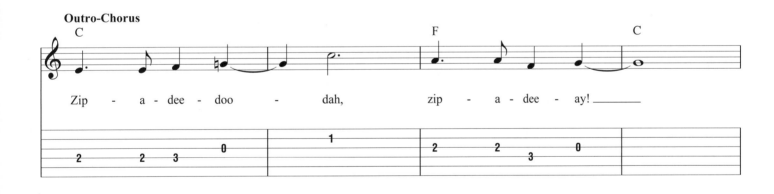

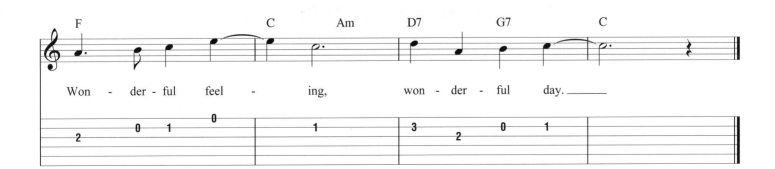

GUITAR NOTATION LEGEND

THE MUSICAL STAFF shows pitches and rhythms and is divided by bar lines into measures. Pitches are named after the first seven letters of the alphabet.

TABLATURE graphically represents the guitar fingerboard. Each horizontal line represents a string, and each number represents a fret.

4th string, 2nd fret · 1st & 2nd strings open, played together · open D chord

HALF-STEP BEND: Strike the note and bend up 1/2 step.

WHOLE-STEP BEND: Strike the note and bend up one step.

GRACE NOTE BEND: Strike the note and immediately bend up as indicated.

SLIGHT (MICROTONE) BEND: Strike the note and bend up 1/4 step.

BEND AND RELEASE: Strike the note and bend up as indicated, then release back to the original note. Only the first note is struck.

PRE-BEND: Bend the note as indicated, then strike it.

VIBRATO: The string is vibrated by rapidly bending and releasing the note with the fretting hand.

PALM MUTING: The note is partially muted by the pick hand lightly touching the string(s) just before the bridge.

HAMMER-ON: Strike the first (lower) note with one finger, then sound the higher note (on the same string) with another finger by fretting it without picking.

PULL-OFF: Place both fingers on the notes to be sounded. Strike the first note and without picking, pull the finger off to sound the second (lower) note.

LEGATO SLIDE: Strike the first note and then slide the same fret-hand finger up or down to the second note. The second note is not struck.

SHIFT SLIDE: Same as legato slide, except the second note is struck.

TRILL: Very rapidly alternate between the notes indicated by continuously hammering on and pulling off.

TAPPING: Hammer ("tap") the fret indicated with the pick-hand index or middle finger and pull off to the note fretted by the fret hand.

NATURAL HARMONIC: Strike the note while the fret-hand lightly touches the string directly over the fret indicated.

PINCH HARMONIC: The note is fretted normally and a harmonic is produced by adding the edge of the thumb or the tip of the index finger of the pick hand to the normal pick attack.

TREMOLO PICKING: The note is picked as rapidly and continuously as possible.

VIBRATO BAR DIVE AND RETURN: The pitch of the note or chord is dropped a specified number of steps (in rhythm), then returned to the original pitch.

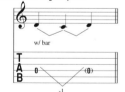

VIBRATO BAR SCOOP: Depress the bar just before striking the note, then quickly release the bar.

VIBRATO BAR DIP: Strike the note and then immediately drop a specified number of steps, then release back to the original pitch.

Additional Musical Definitions

(accent)	•	Accentuate note (play it louder).
(staccato)	•	Play the note short.
D.S. al Coda	•	Go back to the sign (%), then play until the measure marked "*To Coda*," then skip to the section labelled "**Coda**."
D.C. al Fine	•	Go back to the beginning of the song and play until the measure marked "*Fine*" (end).

Fill
• Label used to identify a brief melodic figure which is to be inserted into the arrangement.

N.C.
• Harmony is implied.

• Repeat measures between signs.

• When a repeated section has different endings, play the first ending only the first time and the second ending only the second time.

FIRST 50

Books in the First 50 series contain easy to intermediate arrangements for must-know songs.
Each arrangement is simple and streamlined, yet still captures the essence of the tune.

First 50 Baroque Pieces
You Should Play on Guitar

Includes selections by Johann Sebastian Bach, Robert de Visée, Ernst Gottlieb Baron, Santiago de Murcia, Antonio Vivaldi, Sylvius Leopold Weiss, and more.
00322567....................................$14.99

First 50 Bluegrass Solos
You Should Play on Guitar

I Am a Man of Constant Sorrow • Long Journey Home • Molly and Tenbrooks • Old Joe Clark • Rocky Top • Salty Dog Blues • and more.
00298574....................................$16.99

First 50 Blues Songs
You Should Play on Guitar

All Your Love (I Miss Loving) • Bad to the Bone • Born Under a Bad Sign • Dust My Broom • Hoodoo Man Blues • Little Red Rooster • Love Struck Baby • Pride and Joy • Smoking Gun • Still Got the Blues • The Thrill Is Gone • You Shook Me • and more.
00235790....................................$17.99

First 50 Blues Turnarounds
You Should Play on Guitar

You'll learn cool turnarounds in the styles of these jazz legends: John Lee Hooker, Robert Johnson, Joe Pass, Jimmy Rogers, Hubert Sumlin, Stevie Ray Vaughan, T-Bone Walker, Muddy Waters, and more.
00277469....................................$14.99

First 50 Chords
You Should Play on Guitar

American Pie • Back in Black • Brown Eyed Girl • Landslide • Let It Be • Riptide • Summer of '69 • Take Me Home, Country Roads • Won't Get Fooled Again • You've Got a Friend • and more.
00300255 Guitar........................$12.99

First 50 Classical Pieces
You Should Play on Guitar

Includes compositions by J.S. Bach, Augustin Barrios, Matteo Carcassi, Domenico Scarlatti, Fernando Sor, Francisco Tárrega, Robert de Visée, Antonio Vivaldi and many more.
00155414....................................$16.99

First 50 Folk Songs
You Should Play on Guitar

Amazing Grace • Down by the Riverside • Home on the Range • I've Been Working on the Railroad • Kumbaya • Man of Constant Sorrow • Oh! Susanna • This Little Light of Mine • When the Saints Go Marching In • The Yellow Rose of Texas • and more.
00235868....................................$16.99

First 50 Guitar Duets
You Should Play

Chopsticks • Clocks • Eleanor Rigby • Game of Thrones Theme • Hallelujah • Linus and Lucy (from A Charlie Brown Christmas) • Memory (from Cats) • Over the Rainbow (from The Wizard of Oz) • Star Wars (Main Theme) • What a Wonderful World • You Raise Me Up • and more.
00319706....................................$14.99

First 50 Jazz Standards
You Should Play on Guitar

All the Things You Are • Body and Soul • Don't Get Around Much Anymore • Fly Me to the Moon (In Other Words) • The Girl from Ipanema (Garota De Ipanema) • I Got Rhythm • Laura • Misty • Night and Day • Satin Summertime • When I Fall in Love • and more.
00198594 Solo Guitar $16.99

First 50 Kids' Songs
You Should Play on Guitar

Do-Re-Mi • Hakuna Matata • Let It Go • My Favorite Things • Puff the Magic Dragon • Take Me Out to the Ball Game • Won't You Be My Neighbor? (It's a Beautiful Day in the Neighborhood) • and more.
00300500....................................$15.99

First 50 Licks
You Should Play on Guitar

Licks presented include the styles of legendary guitarists like Eric Clapton, Buddy Guy, Jimi Hendrix, B.B. King, Randy Rhoads, Carlos Santana, Stevie Ray Vaughan and many more.
00278875 Book/Online Audio..........$14.99

First 50 Riffs
You Should Play on Guitar

All Right Now • Back in Black • Barracuda • Carry on Wayward Son • Crazy Train • La Grange • Layla • Seven Nation Army • Smoke on the Water • Sunday Bloody Sunday • Sunshine of Your Love • Sweet Home Alabama • Working Man • and more.
00277366....................................$14.99

First 50 Rock Songs You Should
Play on Electric Guitar

All Along the Watchtower • Beat It • Brown Eyed Girl • Cocaine • Detroit Rock City • Hallelujah • (I Can't Get No) Satisfaction • Oh, Pretty Woman • Pride and Joy • Seven Nation Army • Should I Stay or Should I Go • Smells like Teen Spirit • Smoke on the Water • When I Come Around • You Really Got Me • and more.
00131159....................................$15.99

First 50 Songs by the Beatles You
Should Play on Guitar

All You Need Is Love • Blackbird • Come Together • Eleanor Rigby • Hey Jude • I Want to Hold Your Hand • Let It Be • Ob-La-Di, Ob-La-Da • She Loves You • Twist and Shout • Yellow Submarine • Yesterday • and more.
00295323....................................$19.99

First 50 Songs
You Should Fingerpick on Guitar

Annie's Song • Blackbird • The Boxer • Classical Gas • Dust in the Wind • Fire and Rain • Greensleeves • Road Trippin' • Shape of My Heart • Tears in Heaven • Time in a Bottle • Vincent (Starry Starry Night) • and more.
00149269....................................$16.99

First 50 Songs You Should
Play on 12-String Guitar

California Dreamin' • Closer to the Heart • Free Fallin' • Give a Little Bit • Hotel California • Leaving on a Jet Plane • Life by the Drop • Over the Hills and Far Away • Solsbury Hill • Space Oddity • Wish You Were Here • You Wear It Well • and more.
00287559....................................$15.99

First 50 Songs You Should Play on
Acoustic Guitar

Against the Wind • Boulevard of Broken Dreams • Champagne Supernova • Every Rose Has Its Thorn • Fast Car • Free Fallin' • Layla • Let Her Go • Mean • One • Ring of Fire • Signs • Stairway to Heaven • Trouble • Wagon Wheel • Yellow • Yesterday • and more.
00131209....................................$16.99

First 50 Songs
You Should Play on Bass

Blister in the Sun • I Got You (I Feel Good) • Livin' on a Prayer • Low Rider • Money • Monkey Wrench • My Generation • Roxanne • Should I Stay or Should I Go • Uptown Funk • What's Going On • With or Without You • Yellow • and more.
00149189....................................$16.99

First 50 Songs
You Should Play on Solo Guitar

Africa • All of Me • Blue Skies • California Dreamin' • Change the World • Crazy • Dream a Little Dream of Me • Every Breath You Take • Hallelujah • Wonderful Tonight • Yesterday • You Raise Me Up • Your Song • and more.
00288843....................................$17.99

First 50 Songs
You Should Strum on Guitar

American Pie • Blowin' in the Wind • Daughter • Hey, Soul Sister • Home • I Will Wait • Losing My Religion • Mrs. Robinson • No Woman No Cry • Peaceful Easy Feeling • Rocky Mountain High • Sweet Caroline • Teardrops on My Guitar • Wonderful Tonight • and more.
00148996 Guitar.........................$16.99

HAL•LEONARD®
www.halleonard.com

1022
014

easy GUITAR play along

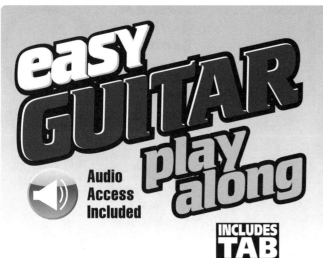

Audio Access Included

INCLUDES TAB

The *Easy Guitar Play Along*® series features streamlined transcriptions of your favorite songs. Just follow the tab, listen to the audio to hear how the guitar should sound, and then play along using the backing tracks. Playback tools are provided for slowing down the tempo without changing pitch and looping challenging parts. The melody and lyrics are included in the book so that you can sing or simply follow along.

1. ROCK CLASSICS
Jailbreak • Living After Midnight • Mississippi Queen • Rocks Off • Runnin' Down a Dream • Smoke on the Water • Strutter • Up Around the Bend.
00702560 Book/CD Pack....... $14.99

2. ACOUSTIC TOP HITS
About a Girl • I'm Yours • The Lazy Song • The Scientist • 21 Guns • Upside Down • What I Got • Wonderwall.
00702569 Book/CD Pack....... $14.99

3. ROCK HITS
All the Small Things • Best of You • Brain Stew (The Godzilla Remix) • Californication • Island in the Sun • Plush • Smells Like Teen Spirit • Use Somebody.
00702570 Book/CD Pack....... $14.99

4. ROCK 'N' ROLL
Blue Suede Shoes • I Get Around • I'm a Believer • Jailhouse Rock • Oh, Pretty Woman • Peggy Sue • Runaway • Wake Up Little Susie.
00702572 Book/CD Pack....... $14.99

6. CHRISTMAS SONGS
Have Yourself a Merry Little Christmas • A Holly Jolly Christmas • The Little Drummer Boy • Run Rudolph Run • Santa Claus Is Comin' to Town • Silver and Gold • Sleigh Ride • Winter Wonderland.
00101879 Book/CD Pack......... $14.99

7. BLUES SONGS FOR BEGINNERS
Come On (Part 1) • Double Trouble • Gangster of Love • I'm Ready • Let Me Love You Baby • Mary Had a Little Lamb • San-Ho-Zay • T-Bone Shuffle.
00103235 Book/ Online Audio..........$17.99

9. ROCK SONGS FOR BEGINNERS
Are You Gonna Be My Girl • Buddy Holly • Everybody Hurts • In Bloom • Otherside • The Rock Show • Santa Monica • When I Come Around.
00103255 Book/CD Pack.....$14.99

10. GREEN DAY
Basket Case • Boulevard of Broken Dreams • Good Riddance (Time of Your Life) • Holiday • Longview • 21 Guns • Wake Me up When September Ends • When I Come Around.
00122322 Book/ Online Audio........$16.99

11. NIRVANA
All Apologies • Come As You Are • Heart Shaped Box • Lake of Fire • Lithium • The Man Who Sold the World • Rape Me • Smells Like Teen Spirit.
00122325 Book/ Online Audio........ $17.99

13. AC/DC
Back in Black • Dirty Deeds Done Dirt Cheap • For Those About to Rock (We Salute You) • Hells Bells • Highway to Hell • Rock and Roll Ain't Noise Pollution • T.N.T. • You Shook Me All Night Long.
14042895 Book/ Online Audio........ $17.99

14. JIMI HENDRIX – SMASH HITS
All Along the Watchtower • Can You See Me • Crosstown Traffic • Fire • Foxey Lady • Hey Joe • Manic Depression • Purple Haze • Red House • Remember • Stone Free • The Wind Cries Mary.
00130591 Book/ Online Audio........$24.99

HAL•LEONARD®

www.halleonard.com

Prices, contents, and availability subject to change without notice.

EASY GUITAR WITH NOTES & TAB

This series features simplified arrangements with notes, tab, chord charts, and strum and pick patterns.

MIXED FOLIOS

00702287	Acoustic	$19.99
00702002	Acoustic Rock Hits for Easy Guitar	$17.99
00702166	All-Time Best Guitar Collection	$29.99
00702232	Best Acoustic Songs for Easy Guitar	$16.99
00119835	Best Children's Songs	$16.99
00703055	The Big Book of Nursery Rhymes & Children's Songs	$16.99
00698978	Big Christmas Collection	$19.99
00702394	Bluegrass Songs for Easy Guitar	$15.99
00289632	Bohemian Rhapsody	$19.99
00703387	Celtic Classics	$16.99
00224808	Chart Hits of 2016-2017	$14.99
00267383	Chart Hits of 2017-2018	$14.99
00334293	Chart Hits of 2019-2020	$16.99
00403479	Chart Hits of 2021-2022	$16.99
00702149	Children's Christian Songbook	$9.99
00702028	Christmas Classics	$9.99
00101779	Christmas Guitar	$16.99
00702141	Classic Rock	$8.95
00159642	Classical Melodies	$12.99
00253933	Disney/Pixar's Coco	$19.99
00702203	CMT's 100 Greatest Country Songs	$34.99
00702283	The Contemporary Christian Collection	$16.99
00196954	Contemporary Disney	$19.99
00702239	Country Classics for Easy Guitar	$24.99
00702257	Easy Acoustic Guitar Songs	$17.99
00702041	Favorite Hymns for Easy Guitar	$12.99
00222701	Folk Pop Songs	$19.99
00126894	Frozen	$14.99
00333922	Frozen 2	$14.99
00702286	Glee	$16.99
00702160	The Great American Country Songbook	$19.99
00702148	Great American Gospel for Guitar	$14.99
00702050	Great Classical Themes for Easy Guitar	$9.99
00148030	Halloween Guitar Songs	$17.99
00702273	Irish Songs	$14.99
00192503	Jazz Classics for Easy Guitar	$16.99
00702275	Jazz Favorites for Easy Guitar	$17.99
00702274	Jazz Standards for Easy Guitar	$19.99
00702162	Jumbo Easy Guitar Songbook	$24.99
00232285	La La Land	$16.99
00702258	Legends of Rock	$14.99
00702189	MTV's 100 Greatest Pop Songs	$34.99
00702272	1950s Rock	$16.99
00702271	1960s Rock	$16.99
00702270	1970s Rock	$24.99
00702269	1980s Rock	$16.99
00702268	1990s Rock	$24.99
00369043	Rock Songs for Kids	$14.99
00109725	Once	$14.99
00702187	Selections from O Brother Where Art Thou?	$19.99
00702178	100 Songs for Kids	$16.99
00702515	Pirates of the Caribbean	$17.99
00702125	Praise and Worship for Guitar	$14.99
00287930	Songs from A Star Is Born, The Greatest Showman, La La Land, and More Movie Musicals	$16.99
00702285	Southern Rock Hits	$12.99
00156420	Star Wars Music	$16.99
00121535	30 Easy Celtic Guitar Solos	$16.99
00244654	Top Hits of 2017	$14.99
00283786	Top Hits of 2018	$14.99
00302269	Top Hits of 2019	$14.99
00355779	Top Hits of 2020	$14.99
00374083	Top Hits of 2021	$16.99
00702294	Top Worship Hits	$17.99
00702255	VH1's 100 Greatest Hard Rock Songs	$39.99
00702175	VH1's 100 Greatest Songs of Rock and Roll	$34.99
00702253	Wicked	$12.99

ARTIST COLLECTIONS

00702267	AC/DC for Easy Guitar	$17.99
00156221	Adele – 25	$16.99
00396889	Adele – 30	$19.99
00702040	Best of the Allman Brothers	$16.99
00702865	J.S. Bach for Easy Guitar	$15.99
00702169	Best of The Beach Boys	$16.99
00702292	The Beatles — 1	$22.99
00125796	Best of Chuck Berry	$16.99
00702201	The Essential Black Sabbath	$15.99
00702250	blink-182 — Greatest Hits	$19.99
02501615	Zac Brown Band — The Foundation	$19.99
02501621	Zac Brown Band — You Get What You Give	$16.99
00702043	Best of Johnny Cash	$19.99
00702090	Eric Clapton's Best	$16.99
00702086	Eric Clapton — from the Album Unplugged	$17.99
00702202	The Essential Eric Clapton	$19.99
00702053	Best of Patsy Cline	$17.99
00222697	Very Best of Coldplay – 2nd Edition	$17.99
00702229	The Very Best of Creedence Clearwater Revival	$16.99
00702145	Best of Jim Croce	$16.99
00702278	Crosby, Stills & Nash	$12.99
14042809	Bob Dylan	$15.99
00702276	Fleetwood Mac — Easy Guitar Collection	$17.99
00139462	The Very Best of Grateful Dead	$17.99
00702136	Best of Merle Haggard	$19.99
00702227	Jimi Hendrix — Smash Hits	$19.99
00702288	Best of Hillsong United	$12.99
00702236	Best of Antonio Carlos Jobim	$15.99
00702245	Elton John — Greatest Hits 1970–2002	$19.99
00129855	Jack Johnson	$17.99
00702204	Robert Johnson	$16.99
00702234	Selections from Toby Keith — 35 Biggest Hits	$12.95
00702003	Kiss	$16.99
00702216	Lynyrd Skynyrd	$17.99
00702182	The Essential Bob Marley	$17.99
00146081	Maroon 5	$14.99
00121925	Bruno Mars – Unorthodox Jukebox	$12.99
00702248	Paul McCartney — All the Best	$14.99
00125484	The Best of MercyMe	$12.99
00702209	Steve Miller Band — Young Hearts (Greatest Hits)	$12.95
00124167	Jason Mraz	$15.99
00702096	Best of Nirvana	$17.99
00702211	The Offspring — Greatest Hits	$17.99
00138026	One Direction	$17.99
00702030	Best of Roy Orbison	$17.99
00702144	Best of Ozzy Osbourne	$14.99
00702279	Tom Petty	$17.99
00102911	Pink Floyd	$17.99
00702139	Elvis Country Favorites	$19.99
00702293	The Very Best of Prince	$22.99
00699415	Best of Queen for Guitar	$16.99
00109279	Best of R.E.M.	$14.99
00702208	Red Hot Chili Peppers — Greatest Hits	$19.99
00198960	The Rolling Stones	$17.99
00174793	The Very Best of Santana	$16.99
00702196	Best of Bob Seger	$16.99
00146046	Ed Sheeran	$19.99
00702252	Frank Sinatra — Nothing But the Best	$12.99
00702010	Best of Rod Stewart	$17.99
00702049	Best of George Strait	$17.99
00702259	Taylor Swift for Easy Guitar	$15.99
00359800	Taylor Swift – Easy Guitar Anthology	$24.99
00702260	Taylor Swift — Fearless	$14.99
00139727	Taylor Swift — 1989	$19.99
00115960	Taylor Swift — Red	$16.99
00253667	Taylor Swift — Reputation	$17.99
00702290	Taylor Swift — Speak Now	$16.99
00232849	Chris Tomlin Collection – 2nd Edition	$14.99
00702226	Chris Tomlin — See the Morning	$12.95
00148643	Train	$14.99
00702427	U2 — 18 Singles	$19.99
00702108	Best of Stevie Ray Vaughan	$17.99
00279005	The Who	$14.99
00702123	Best of Hank Williams	$15.99
00194548	Best of John Williams	$14.99
00702228	Neil Young — Greatest Hits	$17.99
00119133	Neil Young — Harvest	$16.99

Prices, contents and availability subject to change without notice.

Visit Hal Leonard online at halleonard.com

STRUM & SING

The Strum & Sing series for guitar and ukulele provides an unplugged and pared-down approach to your favorite songs – just the chords and the lyrics, with nothing fancy. These easy-to-play arrangements are designed for both aspiring and professional musicians.

GUITAR

Acoustic Classics
00191891 ....$15.99

Adele
00159855 ....$12.99

Sara Bareilles
00102354 ....$12.99

The Beatles
00172234 ....$17.99

Blues
00159335 ....$12.99

Zac Brown Band
02501620 ....$19.99

Colbie Caillat
02501725 ....$14.99

Campfire Folk Songs
02500686 ....$15.99

Chart Hits of 2014-2015
00142554 ....$12.99

Chart Hits of 2015-2016
00156248 ....$12.99

Best of Kenny Chesney
00142457 ....$14.99

Christmas Carols
00348351 ....$14.99

Christmas Songs
00171332 ....$14.99

Kelly Clarkson
00146384 ....$14.99

Coffeehouse Songs for Guitar
00285991 ....$14.99

Leonard Cohen
00265489 ....$14.99

Dear Evan Hansen
00295108 ....$16.99

John Denver Collection
02500632 ....$17.99

Disney
00233900 ....$17.99

Eagles
00157994 ....$14.99

Easy Acoustic Songs
00125478 ....$19.99

Billie Eilish
00363094 ....$14.99

The Five-Chord Songbook
02501718 ....$14.99

Folk Rock Favorites
02501669 ....$14.99

Folk Songs
02501482 ....$14.99

The Four-Chord Country Songbook
00114936 ....$15.99

The Four Chord Songbook
02501533 ....$14.99

Four Chord Songs
00249581 ....$16.99

The Greatest Showman
00278383 ....$14.99

Hamilton
00217116 ....$15.99

Jack Johnson
02500858 ....$19.99

Robert Johnson
00191890 ....$12.99

Carole King
00115243 ....$10.99

Best of Gordon Lightfoot
00139393 ....$15.99

Dave Matthews Band
02501078 ....$10.95

John Mayer
02501636 ....$19.99

The Most Requested Songs
02501748 ....$16.99

Jason Mraz
02501452 ....$14.99

**Tom Petty –
Wildflowers & All the Rest**
00362682 ....$14.99

Elvis Presley
00198890 ....$12.99

Queen
00218578 ....$12.99

Rock Around the Clock
00103625 ....$12.99

Rock Ballads
02500872 ....$9.95

Rocketman
00300469 ....$17.99

Ed Sheeran
00152016 ....$14.99

The Six-Chord Songbook
02502277 ....$17.99

Chris Stapleton
00362625 ....$19.99

Cat Stevens
00116827 ....$17.99

Taylor Swift
00159856 ....$14.99

The Three-Chord Songbook
00211634 ....$12.99

Top Christian Hits
00156331 ....$12.99

Top Hits of 2016
00194288 ....$12.99

Keith Urban
00118558 ....$14.99

The Who
00103667 ....$12.99

Yesterday
00301629 ....$14.99

Neil Young – Greatest Hits
00138270 ....$15.99

UKULELE

The Beatles
00233899 ....$16.99

Colbie Caillat
02501731 ....$10.99

Coffeehouse Songs
00138238 ....$14.99

John Denver
02501694 ....$17.99

The 4-Chord Ukulele Songbook
00114331 ....$16.99

Jack Johnson
02501702 ....$19.99

John Mayer
02501706 ....$10.99

The Most Requested Songs
02501453 ....$15.99

Jason Mraz
02501753 ....$14.99

Pop Songs for Kids
00284415 ....$16.99

Sing-Along Songs
02501710 ....$16.99

HAL•LEONARD®
halleonard.com
Visit our website to see full song lists
or order from your favorite retailer.

*Prices, contents and availability
subject to change without notice.*